OLD TESTAMENT GUIDES

General Editor
R.N. Whybray

1 & 2 KINGS

1 & 2 KINGS

Iain W. Provan

Sheffield Academic Press

To New College students, past and present

Copyright © 1997 Sheffield Academic Press

Published by Sheffield Academic Press Ltd
Mansion House
19 Kingfield Road
Sheffield S11 9AS
England

Printed on acid-free paper in Great Britain
by The Cromwell Press
Melksham, Wiltshire

British Library Cataloguing in Publication Data

A catalogue record for this book is available
from the British Library

ISBN 1-85075-802-6

Contents

Preface

I have discovered to my surprise that what was conceived of around 1982 as only a brief flirtation with the book of Kings has developed into a long-term relationship. A postgraduate dissertation has given way to further teaching and research, which in turn has led to a commentary and to this Old Testament Guide. Parties change in the course of relationships. New perspectives arise. My perspective on Kings is certainly not what it was in 1982, nor even in 1988, when my dissertation was published. My pilgrimage with the book has, in fact, coincided with a general sea-change in the way that Old Testament narrative texts are read among many of those who read them in academic contexts. This makes for an interesting life. It also creates certain difficulties in writing an Old Testament guide—how to balance the traditional and the new, where to place the emphasis, and so on. This volume attempts to introduce the reader to a fairly broad range of issues which arise in relation to Kings, in the context of the kinds of issues which arise in relation to biblical narrative in general. I do not claim to present an exhaustive account of readerly concerns; nor have I attempted to disguise the conclusions at which I have arrived in the course of my pilgrimage. What I have tried to do is to show, in relation to the issues I have addressed, why different readers read Kings differently. Reflection on these fundamental issues should enable readers to form their own judgments on the matters under discussion, and to move beyond these to other matters which may be of interest to them. It should be noted that I have not included in the guide the extensive outline of the contents of the biblical book under consideration which is to be found in some other volumes in the series. If the first-time reader of Kings feels the need of an overview, a brief summary is to be found at the beginning of chapter 5.

Various people must be thanked for their participation in the process of composition. Phil Long, Gordon McConville, Walter Moberly and Francis Watson all read the final draft of the manuscript and offered perceptive advice and criticism. I count myself privileged to be a part of such a supportive academic community. Two New College students, Alan Hall and Mark Nicholas, offered a student perspective on the manuscript, and made valuable comment from that point of view. While naturally exonerating all these readers from complicity in the final product, which they will not have seen before publication, I am most grateful to all of them for their help in making this book what I trust is a readable, informative and stimulating volume.

Iain Provan
New College, Edinburgh

Abbreviations

AB	Anchor Bible
AOAT	Alter Orient und Altes Testament
ATD	Altes Testament Deutsch
B. Bat.	*Baba Bathra*
Bib	*Biblica*
BSem	The Biblical Seminar
BZAW	Beihefte zur *Zeitschrift für die alttestamentliche Wissenschaft*
DSB	Daily Study Bible
FCI	Foundations of Contemporary Interpretation
FOTL	Forms of the Old Testament Literature
Hb.	Hebrew
IBC	Interpretation: A Bible Commentary for Teaching and Preaching
ICT	Issues in Contemporary Theology
ITC	International Theological Commentary
JBL	*Journal of Biblical Literature*
JSOT	*Journal for the Study of the Old Testament*
JSOTS	Journal for the Study of the Old Testament Supplements
MT	Masoretic Text
NCB	New Century Bible
NIBC	New International Biblical Commentary
OBS	The Oxford Bible Series
OTG	Old Testament Guides
OTL	Old Testament Library
OTS	Oudtestamentische Studien
RSV	Revised Standard Version
SHANE	Studies in the History of the Ancient Near East
TynBul	*Tyndale Bulletin*
TC	Tyndale Commentaries
ThSt	Theological Studies
VT	Vetus Testamentum
VTSup	Vetus Testamentum Supplements
WBC	Word Biblical Commentary
WBT	Word Biblical Themes

Select List of Commentaries

A.G. Auld, *Kings* (DSB; Edinburgh: Saint Andrew, 1986). A brief but highly readable book, and a good place for beginners to begin.

C.F. Burney, *Notes on the Hebrew Text of the Books of Kings* (Oxford: Clarendon Press, 1903). A useful resource for readers of the Hebrew text.

M. Cogan and H. Tadmor, *2 Kings* (AB; Garden City, NY: Doubleday, 1988). A large volume whose strength lies in its treatment of the historical background against which the story in 2 Kings is told.

S.J. DeVries, *1 Kings* (WBC; Waco, TX: Word Books, 1985). Commentaries in this series are always a useful resource, not least in their provision of easily comprehensible textual notes and full reading lists on individual chapters.

J. Gray, *1 & 2 Kings* (OTL; London: SCM Press, 3rd edn, 1977). A little dated now, but still useful in its treatment of linguistic, textual, historical and geographical matters.

T.R. Hobbs, *2 Kings* (WBC; Waco, TX: Word Books, 1985). This volume adds to the general strengths of the series an unusual degree of attention to the narrative in itself, and is very helpful in this respect.

G.H. Jones, *1 and 2 Kings* (NCB; 2 vols.; Grand Rapids: Eerdmans, 1984). One of the better commentaries with respect to matters of source, composition and general introductory matters, with full bibliographies.

B.O. Long, *1 Kings, with an Introduction to Historical Literature* (FOTL; Grand Rapids: Eerdmans, 1984); and *2 Kings* (FOTL; Grand Rapids: Eerdmans, 1991). A good place to begin in studying Kings, illuminating discussion being accompanied by full bibliographies indicating further reading.

R.D. Nelson, *First and Second Kings* (IBC; Louisville: John Knox, 1987). One of the best commentaries with respect to the shape of the narrative and its theology, though not designed for verse-by-verse exegesis of the text.

I.W. Provan, *1 and 2 Kings* (NIBC; Peabody: Hendrickson, 1995). A volume devoted entirely to reading Kings as theological narrative within the context of the Christian Bible.

G. Rice, *1 Kings: Nations under God* (ITC; Grand Rapids: Eerdmans, 1990). A brief commentary whose emphasis lies on the theology of the book.

D.J. Wiseman, *1 and 2 Kings* (TC; Leicester: Inter-Varsity Press, 1993). A brief commentary whose strengths lie in its treatment of historical matters, but which unfortunately contains some errors of fact with regard to both text and Old Testament scholarship.

E. Würthwein, *Die Bücher der Könige: Das erste Buch der Könige, Kapitel 1-16* (ATD; Göttingen: Vandenhoek and Ruprecht, 1977); and *Die Bucher der Könige: 1 Kön. 17-2 Kön 25* (ATD; Göttingen: Vandenhoek and Ruprecht, 1984). The best of the German-language commentaries.

1

INTRODUCTION

The first and second 'books' of Kings, as they are often described, represent two parts of what must clearly be thought of (in view of the artificial break between the parts in the midst of the account of Ahaziah's reign in 1 Kgs 22.51 [MT 22.52]–2 Kgs 1.18) as one book. Kings will consequently be referred to throughout this guide as 'the book' rather than 'the books' of Kings (see Gray 1977: 1, for some helpful comments on the division of the book).

The book of Kings is a book which comes to us from the distant past. What kind of book is it? Experience as a teacher suggests that the best place to begin in answering that question (strange as it may seem) might be with other books more familiar to many modern readers of literature: with A.A. Milne's children's classics, *Winnie-The-Pooh* and *The House at Pooh Corner*. The reasons for this somewhat bizarre choice of starting point will become clear in due course.

1. Reading Winnie-The-Pooh

In a famous collection of essays (1967), Frederick Crews offers a number of readings of the Pooh stories from various points of view. For example, the essay entitled 'A Bourgeois Writer's Proletarian Fables', written under the name of Martin Tempralis (1967: 15-26), argues that the stories are political works, which betray their author's bourgeois leanings. It is hardly accidental, Tempralis maintains,

that all the chief actors are property owners with no apparent
necessity to work; that they are supplied as if by miracle with end-
less supplies of honey, condensed milk, balloons, popguns and
extract of malt; and that they crave meaningless aristocratic distinctions and will resort to any measure in their drive for class
prestige. Not for nothing is the sycophant Pooh eventually
invested by Christopher Robin as 'Sir Pooh de Bear, most faithful
of all my knights'. It is a worthy ending to a series of tales in
which every…detail that might suggest some flaw in the capitalist
paradise of pure inherited income has been ruthlessly suppressed.

Only in the old sign (TRESPASSERS W) beside Piglet's
house do we glimpse the truth that this community of para-
sites is kept together through armed intimidation of the proletariat. Piglet's facetious exegesis of this as a shortened
form of his grandfather's name (TRESPASSERS WILLIAM)
only reminds us more pointedly of the hereditary handing-on
of property.

There is, however, another light in which the author's representation of life should be regarded; for the unconscious
meaning of the Pooh stories, argues Tempralis, is quite different from its conscious, intended meaning. The social facts
speak for themselves in spite of all determined effort to deny
their meaning. In fact, dialectical materialism, scientific
socialism, the spirit of the Commune, democratic cooperation
between peoples, and the necessity of revolution are implicitly urged upon us in the stories. The author unwittingly por-
trays his society's rottenness and points the way to its
imminent overthrow. Consider the following:

> It was going to be one of Rabbit's busy days. As soon as he woke up
> he felt important, as if everything depended upon him. It was just
> the day for Organizing Something, or for Writing a Notice Signed
> Rabbit, or for Seeing What Everybody Else Thought About It. It
> was a perfect morning for hurrying round to Pooh, and saying,
> 'Very well, then, I'll tell Piglet', and then going to Piglet, and say-
> ing, 'Pooh thinks—but perhaps I'd better see Owl first'. It was a
> Captainish sort of day, when everybody said, 'Yes, Rabbit', and
> 'No, Rabbit', and waited until he had told them.

Rabbit is the capitalist manager par excellence, a 'captain of
industry' intent upon imposing his will on everyone around
him. 'Just the day for…Writing a Notice Signed Rabbit!' Here
in a nutshell is a complete character study of the exploiter of
labour, writing bureaucratic and imperious notices, pretend-

ing that his arbitrary decisions have been democratically reached ('Pooh thinks—but perhaps I'd better see Owl first'), and demanding an automatic yes or no to each of his commands and rhetorical questions. The interesting point is that this caricature of the bourgeois is implicitly ridiculed by the plot of this story itself. Try as he may to organize his acquaintances, Rabbit never quite succeeds, for they employ the classic defences of the disinherited proletariat when subjected to the exhortations of their rulers. Christopher Robin, for example, pretends to be elsewhere. There is an atmosphere of potential revolt in this chapter which is nothing short of inspiring. No less instructive is the story 'Pooh goes Visiting', in which Rabbit, having deceitfully offered Pooh admittance to sample his overstocked larder, artfully traps his victim in the doorway of his house and exploits him as an unsalaried towel rack. Only the united efforts of a Marxist-Leninist band of workers succeed in extricating Pooh from his servitude.

Of course, Tempralis continues, the symbolic roles of the characters do not remain absolutely static from one story to the next. For example, Pooh, who represents the workers' cause in the examples just given, is himself cast as a capitalist in the 'Piglet Meets a Heffalump' chapter. He and Piglet, joint partners in the imperialist venture of bringing back a live Heffalump, fall out over the question of who is to supply the capital (the acorns or honey to set the trap) and who is to do the manual labour of pit-digging. The solution, naturally, is that the smaller and weaker Piglet is issued with a shovel and put to work. The drawing in the story of Piglet-as-miner, looking upward with a mixture of fatigue and resentment as his exacting supervisor arrives with the honey, is a touching one.

To sum up, the world of Pooh is a world of sheer animalism, where the inhuman bestiality of the free market has full sway. In this unconsciously revealing portrait of capitalism we also glimpse, however, the possibility of a better life—of the forthcoming heroic revolution of oppressed peoples establishing free democratic socialist communes of brotherly peace-loving workers who will march side by side down the collective road to prosperity and equality for all. This optimistic note is what rescues the Pooh stories from decadence, and makes them after all suitable reading for progressive children everywhere.

2. Readers and Texts in General

It may be that we have arrived at a time and a place where readers can no longer recognize humour in texts unless it jumps out and accosts them. If that is the case, let me hasten to reassure readers of this volume that the Marxist reading of the Pooh stories just described is not meant seriously. Humour is indeed intended. If it has been missed, that is probably because the reader either does not know the stories well enough to judge accurately the extent to which Tempralis's account of them represents a preposterous misreading; or does not believe that texts themselves constrain readers to interpret them in certain ways, and therefore does not allow that such things as 'misreadings' truly exist. The remedy for the first complaint is straightforward enough, and involves a more creatively constructed reading list. The second complaint is unlikely to have been contracted in a serious form outside the confines of a modern university campus, since the virus which causes it can only survive in quite rarefied atmospheres (e.g. in departments of English Literature or Biblical Studies). It may be regarded as a kind of temporary insanity (sometimes corporate and institutional) induced by deliberate or unnoticed detachment from intuitive common sense. The remedy involves getting back in touch with the said intuitive common sense, remembering that we all constantly assume that texts possess intentions and meanings which can indeed be misconstrued (e.g. 'Poison: Do Not Drink') and that we regard our first task as interpreters as understanding what those intentions and meanings are (not least because it is sometimes dangerous to fail to do this). It will help in the patient's cure to note that even the most passionate advocates of reader-centred approaches to texts (or 'Humpty Dumpty hermeneutics', as Lewis Carroll might have called it) fall short by some margin of living consistently with this philosophy in their everyday lives, and in particular are no less likely than any author to object if their own texts are 'misread' by others.

We recognize instinctively that the Winnie-the-Pooh stories are not meant to be read in Tempralis's manner. It is this which enables us to read his essay as a humorous piece of work. What he has 'found' in these stories is not what their author had in mind when he wrote them. This is true not only at the level of individual statements in each book, but more fundamentally at the level of the whole book. We recognize that *Winnie-The-Pooh* and *The House at Pooh Corner* are books of children's fiction, and that this is how they should be read. We recognize, in other words, that the question of *genre* is important—that appropriate reading is bound up with the type of literature that a piece of work is. The question of genre is one of the first that we must address in reading any text.

Of course, discovering the genre of a particular text is itself not always without its challenges. While the Pooh stories present us with no difficulty, the same cannot be said, for example, of Jonathan Swift's *Gulliver's Travels*. Here we have a book which might at first appear to the modern reader to be a straightforward children's story, and yet which further enquiry reveals is actually a skilful political satire disguised as a children's story, the style parodying the style of a genre commonly known as 'the travel book'. It is clear that our instincts about genre cannot be entirely trusted, particularly where texts from the past are concerned. Our intuition may on occasion let us down. We are, indeed, capable of making mistakes even with literature of our own time. Orson Welles caused great consternation among the general public in the United States of America, when in 1938 he produced a radio play based on H.G. Wells's famous book, *The War of the Worlds*. Thousands of Americans interpreted the events described according to the genre 'news' rather than the genre 'story'. They believed that a real invasion of Earth by Martians was taking place; and they reacted accordingly, fleeing to the hills, telephoning relatives for one last conversation, and so on. In one famous incident the citizens of a certain town mistook a water tower for a Martian and peppered it with rifle fire. Genre recognition may be important; but it is not always a straightforward matter.

3. Reading the Book of Kings

Even with literature of our own time, we are capable of making mistakes. With slightly older texts, the possibility of error is greater. With ancient texts from the ancient Near East, including Old Testament texts like Kings, the problems are compounded still further. Here our instincts may be quite untrustworthy. The difference in time and culture between ourselves and the original authors is so great that we may initially have entirely improper expectations as to what we are going to find in their work. If this possibility is granted, yet it is also the case that we shall generally have much less information external to the texts to help us in any enquiry about their true nature. Our confidence as to the nature of *Gulliver's Travels* has much to do with the fact that we know a considerable amount about the man who wrote it (e.g. that he was a well-known satirist and a member of the Scriblerus Club, whose purpose was to satirize false learning) and about the conventions which governed its writing (Swift himself claimed it as satire). This is precisely the kind of direct external information which is in short supply in respect of biblical texts like Kings, however much we may find helpful recourse to analogies of one kind or another from the ancient world.

A degree of caution is therefore in order as we approach this text. It is caution inspired by a desire to respect the integrity of the book of Kings, and therefore not to demand that it correspond to our first expectations of it; yet at the same time by an awareness that in the absence of adequate external information, we shall have to try to form an impression of the kind of text it is largely from internal examination. In its very nature the latter course of action runs the risk of subverting the former desire. The interaction between reader and text must therefore be carefully monitored, to ensure that our understanding of the nature of the book is grounded in the book itself, and is not simply a matter of readerly imagination.

What kind of text is Kings? A good place to begin in our search for an answer to this question is surely at the beginning: the opening scenes of the story in 1 Kings 1–2. The narrative which we find here, of course, is itself not so much the beginning of a story as the last chapter of a larger story (the story of David) which has been developing since 1 Samuel 16, and more particularly since 2 Samuel 11. It is in fact the close connection between 2 Samuel and 1 Kings 1–2 that has often led scholars to the view that there is a unified source behind our biblical books at this point (a 'Succession' or 'Court' Narrative). It is in 2 Samuel 11 that the Bathsheba who plays such a prominent role in 1 Kings 1–2 first appears, as the wife of Uriah the Hittite: a wife possessed by David at the cost, first, of Uriah's life (2 Sam. 11.6-27), and then, secondly, of the lives of various of David's sons, as judgment falls on his own house because of his sin (12.1-12). First, the son born to David and Bathsheba dies (12.15-23); then another of David's sons, Amnon, is struck down by Absalom for the crime of rape which he has perpetrated on his half-sister Tamar (2 Sam. 13). Finally, Absalom himself rebels against his father, and is executed by Joab (2 Sam. 18). This sorry tale raises an important question in the reader's mind. The prophet Nathan, himself a major player in the first two chapters of Kings, had earlier promised David that his dynasty would last forever (2 Sam. 7.1-17). David's kingship would not be like Saul's, which all but died with him (1 Sam. 31). Instead, God would raise up one of David's sons and establish his kingdom forever (2 Sam. 7.12-13). How is this promise now to be fulfilled, in view of Nathan's later word of judgment to David in 2 Samuel 12 and its outworking? Where is a surviving son to be found now, to sit on David's throne, as David approaches the time when he will rest with his fathers (2 Sam. 7.12)? It is this question which the first two chapters of the book of Kings resolve, in a narrative which involves many of the main characters from the books of Samuel. Chapter 1 tells us how it came to pass that it was Solomon, and not someone else, who succeeded David; while chapter 2 reports David's last instructions to Solomon, and tells us what Solomon did immediately after David's death to tie up several 'loose ends' from the David story, and thus consolidate his position. The transition from David to Solomon thus described, chapter 3 continues the story of Solomon alone which has begun in 2.12.

a. *The Book of Kings as Historiographical Literature*
What may we deduce from 1 Kings 1–2 about the nature of
the text with which we are dealing? Perhaps the most obvious thing to be said, first of all, is that this is a text which is
interested in the past. At its heart 1 Kings 1–2 concerns two
centrally important figures from Israel's history, and a fundamentally important question about their relationship: how
it is that Solomon is David's legitimate heir? The fate of the
Davidic dynasty is, indeed, a central concern of the remainder of the book as well, as Israel looks back on her monarchic
period and evaluates it from the perspective of exile, when
such 'kings' as remain stand under foreign domination (2 Kgs
25.27-30).

The historiographical impulse which drives the narrative
in Kings is particularly clear from the framework within
which much of the book is constructed. We find a trace of this
framework in 1 Kgs 2.10-11, where we are told that 'David
slept with his fathers and was buried in the city of David.
And the time that David reigned over Israel was forty years;
he reigned seven years in Hebron, and thirty-three years in
Jerusalem'. It is more commonly provided, however, in a
much fuller form. It characteristically informs the reader
when, in relation to another king, a certain monarch came to
the throne; how long he reigned; and the name of his capital
city. It gives us information about his death/burial and his
successor, and tells us where to look for further information
about him. It offers an evaluation of him in terms of his religious policy. In the case of Judean (rather than northern
Israelite) kings, it tells us the name of his mother and his
age at his accession to the throne. A good example of the full
set of 'regnal formulae' (as the various elements of the framework are often called) is to be found in 1 Kgs 22.41-43, 45, 50
(MT 22.41-44, 46, 51). These formulae indicate just how firmly
rooted in what we might term the 'real' world (as opposed to
what some might term a 'fictive' world) the author or authors
of Kings wished their narrative to be. The story concerns
part of the history of Israel. The book of Kings is a text about
the past.

b. *The Book of Kings as Narrative Literature*
This is not to say, of course, that the book is without its
'fictive' elements. It is a story about the *past*; but it is also a
story about the past. The text may clearly seek to tell us
about real events and characters in Israel's history; but it
does this in ways that equally clearly owe as much to narrative artistry and literary convention as to any desire to
describe things 'as they really were'. It is at this point that
modern readers who have been taught to think of 'history' in
a particularly narrow way may find some difficulty with
Kings. What has narrative artistry to do with the task of
describing the past, it may be asked? We shall return to this
important question in due course. For the moment, let us
simply satisfy ourselves that, however problematic it may
seem, the book of Kings is indeed as much narrative as it is
history.

We may begin with the names of some of the characters we
meet in these opening scenes. Names are commonly invested
with a great deal of significance in the Old Testament, and
can function as vehicles through which authors convey something of their own viewpoint. Perhaps the best examples are
provided by those occasions upon which names have deliberately been corrupted, apparently in order to express disgust
for them (for example, 2 Sam. 2.8 and 1 Chron. 8.33, where
the name of the god Baal in Esh-Baal's name has been
replaced by the Hebrew noun *bōšet*, 'shame'). Word-play
using Hebrew names does not, however, stop there, as
1 Kings 1 reveals. At first sight, it may seem unimportant to
the reader unfamiliar with how Hebrew narrative works that
Adonijah spends most of chapter 1 eating, while his world
falls apart around him. Certainly there is a neat irony in the
fact that, while Adonijah imagines that it is David who lacks
the crucial information from outside his small bedroom world
that would enable the king to frustrate his designs, it turns
out to be Adonijah who is fatally ignorant, closeted away
from political reality, wining and dining his friends. There is,
however, even more to it than that. The name of Adonijah's
mother, Haggith, is derived, like several other biblical
Hebrew names, from the verbal root *ḥgg*, from which we also
have the noun *ḥag*, 'a feast' (though this is not the word used

in this verse). The name of Solomon's mother Bathsheba, on the other hand, probably means 'daughter of the oath'. Certainly its second part (*šebaʿ*) is connected with the verbal root *šbʿ*, which in the Niphal conjugation means 'to swear an oath'—the very verb which we find used throughout 1.13-30 (cf. vv. 13, 17, 29, 30), and which reappears in 1.51. While the son of the feast-lady eats, the daughter of the oath succeeds in reminding the king of what he has sworn, and so ensures that Adonijah is dependent for his life upon Solomon keeping his own oath. The story is told in such a way as to make these connections between the mothers and their sons clear, and to invest its characters with a sense of predestination. Naming is intrinsically tied up with the artistry of the narrative.

A different kind of word-play, with different purpose, is found with the use of the Hebrew verb *ydʿ*, 'to know', in 1 Kings 1. The book opens in what at first sight seems a rather puzzling way, with the story of the king and the virgin (1.1-4). The point of the Abishag incident appears to be that it suggests to the watching court, and to Adonijah in particular, that David has lost his virility, and thus his ability to govern. The David of old had not shown himself to be impervious to the charms of beautiful women (1 Sam. 25, especially v. 3; 2 Sam. 11, especially v. 2). Yet in Abishag's case, 'the king knew her not' (*ydʿ*). This is not the only knowledge that David lacks as the story progresses; for we are also later told that he does not know (*ydʿ*) that Adonijah has made himself king (1 Kgs 1.14). Yet this was a king who had possessed the reputation of having 'wisdom like the wisdom of the angel of God to know all things that are on the earth' (2 Sam. 14.20). His lack of 'knowledge' now speaks in powerful terms of a king very much on the decline.

The figure of the son who challenges this ailing, indecisive father is drawn in a quite contrasting way (1 Kgs 1.5-6). Adonijah is the stereotypical hero-figure, the stuff of kings; a decision-maker who grasps the opportunities open to him, gathering the symbols of kingship around him—chariots, horses, and a regiment of soldiers (cf. 1 Sam. 8.11). Yet here, too, there is more going on in the narrative than may at first meet the eye. His military recruitment is reminiscent of the earlier action of his brother Absalom (2 Sam. 15.1), with whom Adonijah is explicitly associated here. Absalom, too, was 'a very handsome man' (2 Sam 14.25-26); and he too was the beneficiary (if that is the term) of parental negligence and indulgence (cf. the picture throughout 2 Sam. 13–18 of a son out of control, and a father who seems unaware of, or uncaring about, what is happening). In associating Adonijah so clearly with Absalom, the author(s) already hint to us that this son, too, is in reality heading for disaster, no matter how promising his prospects appear. In describing him in terms of his physical appearance alone, and omitting any mention of other attributes, the author(s) are not only associating him directly with Absalom, but also, and just as significantly, with Saul (1 Sam. 9.2; 10.23-24). Saul and Absalom are both the kind of hero-figures considered by the people (or many of them) to be royal material. The author(s) of the books of Samuel, however, go out of their way to stress that God looks on the heart, and not on the external appearance of things (1 Sam. 16.7, with its sequel in the story in 1 Sam. 17 of giant Saul's impotence in relation to larger Goliath, contrasted with tiny David's striking success). Adonijah, like Absalom and Saul, is an impressive figure, with all physical prowess on his side. But it will be the enfeebled David who will emerge on top in this encounter also, albeit with help from Nathan and Bathsheba; and the eternal throne will once again be won, as it was before, by one who is described, not merely in terms of his external attributes, but also in terms of what is in his heart and mind (cf. 1 Kgs 3.3-14).

What we have in 1 Kings 1–2, then, is a narrative: a carefully constructed, highly artistic narrative. Those who take the book of Kings seriously must pay as much attention to its character as story as they do to its character as historiography.

c. *The Book of Kings as Didactic Literature*
A third thing suggested to us by the opening chapters of Kings is that the book is not only a narrative about the past, but also a narrative which seeks to *teach* its readers something (or a number of things) about God and God's ways. That is, the book of Kings tells its readers about Israel's past, not so that they should become better informed about it in some

abstract, intellectually detached way, but so that they should
learn from it. This is most clearly signalled in the opening
section of David's parting speech to Solomon, in 1 Kgs 2.1-4.
Like God's words to Joshua upon his 'succession' to the
leadership of Israel after Moses' death (Josh. 1.6-9), David's
words to Solomon open with an injunction to 'be strong' (the
language of warriorship, cf. 1 Sam. 4.9 for the conjunction of
'be strong and be/show yourself a man'), before moving on
immediately to define the framework within which that
strength must be exercised (obedience to God). The exercise
of royal power is not to be arbitrary, for the king is not a law
unto himself. It is rather to be in accordance with the Law of
Moses (2.3, cf. Josh. 1.7, 'all the law my servant Moses gave
you'). Particularly in view here (as in Joshua) is the law code
of Deuteronomy: that is the text to which the language of
verses 3-4, taken cumulatively, points us (e.g. 'observe what
the LORD your God requires', Deut. 11.1; 'walk in his ways',
Deut. 8.6; 'keep his decrees and commands', Deut. 6.2; 'that
you may prosper in all you do', Deut. 29.9; 'that the LORD may
keep his promise', Deut. 9.5; 'with all their heart and soul',
Deut. 4.29). It is Deuteronomic language such as this which
we find recurring again and again in Kings, as first Solomon
himself (1 Kgs 11), then almost all the succeeding kings of
Israel and Judah, are weighed in relation to the Mosaic law
code and found wanting (e.g. Jeroboam, 1 Kgs 12.25-33; 14.1-
16; Ahaz, 2 Kgs 16.1-4). It is this lack of obedience to God
which eventually brings an end to the monarchy and leads
Israel into exile from their land (2 Kgs 17.7-23; 23.26-27;
24.1-4), the righteousness of Josiah notwithstanding (cf.
2 Kgs 22–23, noting the references there to 'the book of the
Law' which guides Josiah's reform, a phrase used in the
Pentateuch only of Deuteronomy: Deut. 28.61; 29.21; 30.10;
31.26; cf. also Josh. 1.8; 8.30-35; 23.6; 24.26).

All this suggests that at least one of the purposes of Kings
is to provide its readers with an explanation of their past in
terms of the theological programme outlined in Deuteronomy,
with a view to promoting that programme in the present. It
is this aspect of Kings, and its connection in this respect with
books like Joshua, which has led Old Testament scholars in
recent times to refer to Joshua, Judges, Samuel and Kings

together as the 'Deuteronomic'/'Deuteronomistic History'. I shall have more to say of this in due course. The idea that these books belong together, however, and have a didactic function is already an old one, encapsulated in the ancient Jewish description of these books as 'The Former Prophets', part of the second division of the Hebrew canon of Scripture ('The Prophets'). However 'prophecy' was precisely understood, it is as a *prophetic*, scriptural book that Kings was received among Jews, and later among Christians. The text came from God and had things to say to the present reader about God and about divine–human relationships. Thus for Josephus (*Antiquities*, 1.14), the main lesson to be learned from the biblical historical sources in general was that those who conform themselves to God's will prosper and those who do not bring disaster upon themselves. For Philo (*On the Confusion of Languages*, 149), those regnal formulae in Kings which evaluate the king in terms of his obedience to God (the so-called 'judgment formulae', for example, 1 Kgs 15.11; 22.43 [MT 22.43-44]) testify to 'souls made immortal by their virtues'. The later Christian writer Bede (in his *Ecclesiastical History*) was heavily influenced by Samuel–Kings in both his understanding of the course of Anglo-Saxon history and in his view of how it should be presented in writing; and these books also played an important part in the formation of European political theory, particularly as it related to the rights and duties of kingship, throughout Bede's period and long after it (cf., e.g., Hobbes, *Leviathan*, 2.20 and 3.42; Locke, *First Treatise on Government*, pp. 159-62).

The reception of the book corresponds to important aspects of its nature. We have in Kings a treatment of Israel's history which is theological and which possesses a didactic purpose. Precisely how that purpose is to be thought of has been a matter of debate; and we shall have to return to consider this matter further. For the moment it is important only to establish that it exists.

4. Conclusion

A preliminary look at the book of Kings suggests, then, that it is literature in narrative form with historiographical and didactic intent. Each of the areas discussed briefly above now requires much closer and more detailed scrutiny, if we are to do justice to the whole. In the second chapter I shall give further consideration, in the first instance, to the book of Kings as narrative.

Further Reading

The general literature mentioned, with connected items:

L. Carroll, *The Annotated Alice: Alice's Adventures in Wonderland and Through the Looking Glass* (Harmondsworth: Penguin, rev. edn, 1970). See ch. 6 of *Through the Looking Glass* for an exploration of 'Humpty Dumpty hermeneutics'.

H. Cantril, *The Invasion from Mars: A Study in the Psychology of Panic, with the Complete Script of the Famous Orson Welles Broadcast* (Princeton: Princeton University Press, 1940)

F. Crews, *The Pooh Perplex: A Student Casebook* (London: Arthur Baker, 1967). An amusing series of essays on the two books below.

A.A. Milne, *Winnie-The-Pooh* (London: Methuen, 1926). The original.

A.A. Milne, *The House at Pooh Corner* (London: Methuen, 1928). The sequel.

J. Swift, *The Annotated Gulliver's Travels* (ed. I. Asimov; New York: Potter, 1980). The classic children's novel—or is it a satire?

H.G. Wells, *The War of the Worlds* (London: Pan Books, 1975). The novel behind the radio broadcast.

Some reading on 1 Kings 1–2 as narrative:

M. Garsiel, 'Puns upon Names as a Literary Device in 1 Kings 1–2', *Bib* 72 (1991), pp. 379-86.

J.S. Ackerman, 'Knowing Good and Evil: A Literary Analysis of the Court History in 2 Samuel 9-20 and 1 Kings 1–2', *JBL* 109 (1990), pp. 41-60.

I.W. Provan, 'Why Barzillai of Gilead (1 Kings 2.7)? Narrative Art and the Hermeneutics of Suspicion in 1 Kings 1–2', *TynBul* 46 (1995), pp. 103-16.

On the 'Succession' or 'Court' Narrative:

R.P. Gordon, *1 and 2 Samuel* (OTG; Sheffield: JSOT Press, 1984), pp. 81-94.

2

THE BOOK OF KINGS
AS NARRATIVE LITERATURE

The book of Kings is *narrative* literature, rather than some other sort (e.g. poetic literature). A story is narrated, involving a number of characters; events follow each other in chronological sequence, from its beginning to its end; and the whole is bound together by verbal and thematic links between its parts. The main characters in the story are the LORD God of Israel, various Israelite kings and prophets, and a number of significant foreigners—although it is not always the main characters who are accorded the most prominence. It is a recurring feature of the Elisha narratives in 2 Kings 3–8, for example, that it is characteristically the humble and lowly who are the channels of God's salvation to Israelite and foreigner alike, rather than those of status and importance. The account of the healing of Naaman in 2 Kings 5 offers a particularly good example of this, in its account of the arrogant army chief who is set and kept on the path to healing by his servants (5.2-3, 13) and ends up as 'a little child' (5.14) under prophetic authority (cf. further Chapter 6).

Narratives commonly have plots. The plot of the book of Kings concerns the attempt that Israel makes under its monarchy (or more often, does not make) to live as the people of God in the promised land, and how God deals with his people in their success and failure. It is a plot worked out gradually, as king succeeds king from David (1 Kgs 1.1) through to Zedekiah (2 Kgs 25.7), with an epilogue reserved for Jehoiachin (25.27-30). It is also a plot worked out in an ordered way, as the reign of each king is situated in the framework with its 'regnal formulae' within which the book is constructed (see Chapter 1.3.a for an account of the framework). These formulae, with their general regularity of expression throughout Kings, not only indicate how firmly rooted in the 'real' world the narrative is intended to be, but also contribute much to the book's sense of narrative coherence—to the sense that it 'hangs together' as a single piece of work (cf., for example, 1 Kgs 14.22-24 with 2 Kgs 16.2-4, and both with 2 Kgs 17.7-11). Ancient tradition ascribed the book, in fact, to a single author—to the prophet Jeremiah (cf. *B. Bat.* 15a).

1. Theories about Authorship, Date and Place

Modern scholarship has, on the whole, doubted the reliability of the above-mentioned tradition. It has generally been doubted whether a single author could have written the whole book at all. Although there is certainly a significant degree of coherence to be found within it, yet (it has been argued) there is a greater or lesser degree of incoherence as well. The book of Kings has features which are unexpected in the work of a single author—inconsistencies, repetitions, variations in style and language, and so on.

For example, there is an obvious inconsistency in 2 Kgs 17.24-41. Here, in the account of the religion of the peoples settled in the land of Israel after the exile of the northern Israelites to Assyria, we are first told that these peoples 'feared the LORD but also served their own gods' (v. 33). Almost immediately, however, this statement is disputed: 'they do not fear the LORD, and they do not follow the statutes...' (v. 34). It is made quite clear that the worship of other gods is incompatible with the worship of the LORD (vv. 35-40). Yet the summary statement of v. 41 appears to return to the perspective of v. 33: 'So these nations feared the LORD, and also served their graven images'. There appear to be two competing views here.

Then again, 2 Kgs 18.9-12 essentially repeats information we already find in 2 Kgs 17.1-6. We are told twice of Shalmaneser's siege of Samaria, of the fall of the city in

Hoshea's ninth year, and of the exile of the Israelites in Halah, and on the Habor, the river of Gozan, and in the cities of the Medes. This kind of repetition requires an explanation.

Finally by way of example, there appear to be differences in style and language between the regnal formulae in the majority of the book of Kings and those in the closing chapters. Nelson (1981) argues that the regnal formulae up until the reign of Jehoahaz of Judah (2 Kgs 23.31-35) display a fascinating diversity within an overall unity of expression. The formulae for the last four kings of Judah, however, are all virtually the same, are shorter than their predecessors, and are not supplemented by additional information. For Nelson, there is a rigidity about these formulae which suggests an imitator of the original author of Kings who lacked his creative flair.

a. *Author and Sources*
Examples like those just described have persuaded the majority of modern scholars that, whatever else may be true about the composition of the book of Kings, at the very least the person who put it together was not a free agent, able to do just as he wished. He was to a greater or lesser extent constrained by the material available to him; and he was unable or unwilling to impose complete consistency upon it. The 'tensions' within the book, on this view, are the result of the straightforward incorporation within it of source materials of differing perspectives. For Martin Noth, for example, who in 1943 published a study of all the books from Deuteronomy to Kings which has proved highly influential in subsequent discussion, the person behind these books—given the name 'Deuteronomist', because of the centrality of Deuteronomy to his thinking, '...did not intend to create something original and of a piece but was at pains to select, compile, arrange and interpret existing traditional material...' That is why '...the separate parts of the work seem disunited and heterogeneous' (Eng. trans. 1981: 77). The Deuteronomist, working in the period after the events described in 2 Kings 24–25 (the exile of Judah from the land), was content to allow his own voice to be heard in the midst of the voices expressed in this 'existing traditional material', occasionally offering more

extended passages of interpretation to help the reader to
grasp his own point of view (e.g. 2 Kgs 17.7-23, which sum-
marizes the history of Israel from a Deuteronomistic point of
view).

The book of Kings itself refers, of course, to sources: 'the
book of the acts of Solomon' (1 Kgs 11.41); and much more
frequently, 'the book of the chronicles of the kings of Israel'
(e.g. 1 Kgs 14.19) and 'the book of the chronicles of the kings
of Judah' (e.g. 1 Kgs 14.29). Even those modern scholars who
have been content to accept that such sources actually
existed have doubted, however, whether they can account for
the variety of the material that we find in Kings. Various
other theories about sources have therefore been put forward. It was the common belief before Noth that the hypothetical Pentateuchal sources J and E continued beyond the
Pentateuch at least into Joshua; and some thought that
these sources extended as far as Kings. Then again, many
have found a 'Court' or 'Succession Narrative' in 2 Samuel,
the final section of which provided the basic material for
1 Kings 1–2; while it is widely accepted that cycles of
prophetic narratives lie behind the presentation of such
prophets as Elijah and Elisha. It is to a great extent the differing character of such sources, it has been alleged, which
has produced the 'unevennesses' that we now find in the
finished product that we are studying.

b. *Text and Editors*
Other Old Testament scholars, however, have not been convinced that all the tensions within a book like Kings can be
explained in terms of the use of source material. Some of
these tensions, it has been argued, imply that the original
work has been expanded by one or more later editors. They,
too, were constrained by what lay before them; and they, too,
were only able to make the text convey their particular message to a certain extent. There are various forms of theory
about secondary editing. The two main lines of thought, however, are that the book of Kings known to us now is an
updated version either of an originally pre-exilic book or of
an originally exilic book.

That the book of Kings is pre-exilic in origin is an older

critical idea which never entirely disappeared, in spite of Noth's hypothesis about Deuteronomy–Kings, and in due course has come to shape for many scholars the way in which Noth's overall thesis is understood. F.M. Cross is widely acknowledged as the leading influence in establishing a school of thought which understands Noth's entire Deuteronomistic History as originally pre-exilic, dating from the reign of king Josiah (cf. 2 Kgs 22–23). For Cross the work was a propaganda document designed to persuade northern Israel to return to Judah and the temple, and to persuade Judah that its restoration to ancient grandeur depended upon the return of the nation to the covenant with the LORD and the return of her king to the ways of David. Its optimistic tone is now rather subdued in the exilic edition by more pessimistic passages such as 2 Kgs 21.2-15, which speak of the inevitability of Judah's condemnation and cloud the earlier distinction between Israel and Judah. These passages represent the perspective of Deuteronomists who have experienced the exile. This view of the composition of the Deuteronomistic History in general and of Kings in particular has proved attractive to Old Testament scholars, particularly in North America, although by no means everyone who has subscribed to a pre-exilic edition of Kings has also thought that the description of Josiah's reign represented the highlight of this original. There has been some support, rather, for the figure of Hezekiah as the original 'hero' of the book.

The second main theory is more German than North American. It is associated in the first instance with the University of Göttingen and the particular figure of R. Smend. On this view, Noth's exilic dating of the Deuteronomistic History (including Kings) is quite correct. However, the original (DtrG) has subsequently been expanded by Deuterononomistic editors who were interested, first of all, in prophecy (DtrP), and secondly in law (DtrN). There is a two-fold redaction of Kings, then, each redaction introducing new emphases. The prophetic redactor introduced such texts as 1 Kgs 14.7-11, 16.1-4, and 21.20b-24, which are concerned with prophecy and fulfilment. The 'nomistic' redactor added passages like 1 Kgs 6.11-13 and

9.1-9, which emphasize the theme of obedience and disobedience and present a more advanced theology of law.

c. *Date and Place*

For most scholars of the modern era, then, what we have in Kings is a composite work, put together over a longer or shorter period of time by a number of authors or editors, its various parts speaking with more or less conflicting voices. The date which scholars give for the book, or at least emphasize as the date of the 'main' work, obviously depends upon which theory about composition is adopted. Although some scholars have argued that there was already a substantial and continuous narrative about the Israelite monarchy as early as the ninth century BCE (e.g. A.F. Campbell), what we might refer to as the 'mainstream' datings of Kings in line with the major theories about composition just discussed would begin with a hypothetical pre-exilic version of the seventh century BCE (e.g. Provan, 1988: 133-55; McKenzie, 1991: 117-34). In its present form, of course, the book could not possibly have been written before the sixth century (cf. the description of Jehoiachin's release in 2 Kgs 25.27-30, which means that this passage could not have been written before 561 BCE), which is precisely when some think it was *first* put together (e.g. Noth, 1981: 79-83). W. Dietrich, working with the Göttingen model, dates DtrG around 580, DtrN around 560, and DtrP at some point in between. Other scholars, however, maintain that Kings is the product of a still later time, and it must be said that there is evidence that at least some reworking of the text has taken place in the Persian period. For example, the intriguing phrase 'governors of the land' in 1 Kgs 10.15 seems best understood in the light of the organization of the Persian empire, when the land described in 4.24 [MT 5.4] as lit. 'Across-The-River' (RSV's 'region west of the Euphrates') was indeed administered on behalf of the Persian emperor by governors (cf. Ezra 8.36; Neh. 2.7, 9). In fact, the Hebrew text's 'kings of the evening' in 10.15 (RSV's 'kings of Arabia') is possibly a poetic reference to kings of the *west* (where the sun sets), the rulers of areas within Solomon's empire. Solomon's wealth, then, comes from revenue deriving from within the empire, as well as from explorers and traders perhaps working outside the empire; but the point is that this reality is described in language which suggests a Persian perspective.

Scholarly opinion on the place of writing also varies. The two main contenders are Palestine and Babylon, with the former clearly being implied on the pre-exilic theory of composition and being favoured also by the majority of those who write of exilic composition or editing. The sources, it is argued, would have been more accessible in Palestine, and the interests of the book are more in Palestine than in Babylon. For example, the idolatrous practices described in Kings are Canaanite rather than Babylonian, while the book is clearly more interested in the destruction of Judah than in the exile.

2. Reading the Book of Kings as Narrative

a. *'Traditional Modern' Reading*
It is hardly surprising, given the general perception of the nature of Kings within the academic community throughout most of the modern period as I have just described it, that scholarly reading of the book *as* a book in this period should generally have ceased. It is not difficult at all to find monographs and articles from this period which hypothesize along the lines mentioned above about the original source material used by the editors of Kings, or about the various levels of editing which might exist in the text. It is not even very difficult to find discussion of the theology or theologies of the various people supposed to have been responsible for the book, as we shall see later (Chapter 5). What is thin on the ground before the last decade or so is writing on the book itself in its final form as a piece of narrative. This is also true of commentaries. There is a plentiful supply of commentaries which tell the reader, on the one hand, what individual pieces of Kings might have meant before they were incorporated into the book; or, on the other, which pieces are 'original' to the book and which are later additions. We may fairly characterize the commentaries of Gray, Jones and DeVries, for example, as those which place emphasis on such matters. Then again, there is no shortage of discussion of the histori-

cal and cultural background of the various parts of Kings; of
the likely geographical location of the various cities mentioned in the text; of the obscurities of Old Testament flora
and fauna. Cogan and Tadmor, and Wiseman, for example,
tend to give great attention to such things. Of the analysis of
bits and pieces there has been (and continues to be) no end.
Of the reading of a reconstructed narrative of some kind—
the text rearranged to make it more 'plausible', and the various 'inconsistent' parts filtered out or subordinated to the
narrative line being pursued by the commentator—there has
been a little. But of the reading of the book as it stands *as a
complete story* there has been, until recently, scarcely any.

This is not surprising, given the widespread conviction
among scholars that the book is not in its fundamental
nature a story in the conventional sense, but a more or less
incoherent combination of sources and redactional layers. It
is unsurprising in particular when we remember that the
predominant interest of many scholarly readers of Old
Testament narrative throughout the modern period has been
in the history which is thought to lie behind the text rather
than in the text itself. There has been a general tendency in
exegetical endeavour, in fact, to view the text more as a
quarry out of which 'facts' are to be mined than as a story
that is to be read—a tendency which is just as evident in
what are generally termed 'conservative' works as it is in any
other sort. It is striking that in Wiseman's recent commentary, for instance, the author spends much more time relating pieces of text to events outside the text, many of which
the text knows nothing of, than he spends explaining the
connection of the various pieces of text *to each other*. The
nature of the text as continuous narrative is simply not
taken seriously when it comes to its interpretation. His comments on 2 Kgs 8.1-6 offer a particularly good example of
this. Apparently we may only say, in spite of its narrative
location, that the incident described here '*may* [my italics]
have taken place in the reign of Jehoram' (1993: 212). What
is going on *behind* the text is regarded as much more important than what is happening *in* it—even though the text may
be viewed as one inspired by God himself. This is only one
example of what has generally been the case in modern read-

ing of Hebrew narrative. The text has all too often been thought to exist only so that it may be peeled away, layer by layer, to reveal historical 'reality'—the coherent entity behind the multi-faceted incoherence of the text.

b. *Newer Narrative Approaches*
The past decade or so, however, has seen something of a challenge to this way of thinking about Hebrew narrative, a challenge with far-reaching implications for the way in which it is read. It has come, perhaps predictably, not from those interested primarily in history, but from those with expertise and broader interests in literature. It is expressed in the first instance in terms of scepticism: scepticism about the assumption of incoherence which is so widely shared by Old Testament exegetes. Is repetition necessarily an indication of multiple sources or editors? Various authors have shown, to the contrary, that repetition in narrative can be understood as an aspect of literary artistry (e.g. Licht, 1978: 51-95; Alter, 1981: 88-113). What of variation in style and language and 'inconsistency'? Can individual authors not vary their style and language for their own particular literary purposes; and what is that which compels us to use the word 'inconsistent' rather than terms such as 'theologically complex' or 'ironic' (cf. Sternberg, 1985: 84-152, 186-320; Gunn and Fewell, 1993: 46-89, 147-73)? Is there anything, in fact, which *compels* us to see incoherence in a book such as Kings? Or is it simply that Old Testament scholars, often lacking general competence in literary matters, and approaching the text with inherited presuppositions about its incoherent nature (among other things), have largely found what they expected to find?

The questioning has been sharp; and traditional modern Old Testament scholarship has often found it difficult to mount a successful rearguard action in attempting to respond to it. The cause has not been helped by the fact that much of the more recent work on Hebrew narrative, which has eschewed speculation about the way in which the biblical texts might have reached their present form, and has attempted to understand them just as they are, has been extraordinarily fruitful in its efforts to make sense of them.

It has revealed the extent of the artistry which has been involved in constructing, not only individual stories, but also whole sections of text and entire books. Incoherence tends to dissolve in the course of such analysis; and models of composition which presuppose frustrated or reluctant authors, not fully in control of their material, or incompetent editors, intruding their presence sufficiently that we should notice them, but unable fully to impose themselves—such models have appeared increasingly implausible. It is more and more difficult, in the light of the evidence, to view the authors of the biblical narrative texts as victims either of their sources or of their own incompetence. It is correspondingly easier to adopt the general hypothesis that, whether they used sources or not, they have presented to us the material which they wished to present, ordered and crafted in the way they wished to do it; that they have produced texts intended to make sense as they are read cumulatively from beginning to end, each part being seen in the context of the whole. This appears to be the assumption with which we approach narrative literature in general. There has increasingly seemed little reason to depart from it in the case of Hebrew narrative literature in particular, and good reason to adopt a commitment, within this general framework, to consider it possible in the first instance that individual 'problems in the text' may actually be 'problems with my understanding of the text' that can be resolved by closer attention to the data.

c. *Problems in Kings Revisited*
We may return with these thoughts in mind to our three particular examples from Kings. Is it possible to understand the 'inconsistency' in 2 Kgs 17.24-41 in a way that is consonant with the general view of Hebrew narrative that has been outlined above? That is, of course, to put the question in a way that invites a somewhat defensive answer. Attack being the best form of defence, however, it might be best to begin rather by drawing attention to the implausibility of the position adopted by those who positively argue for 'competing' voices in this passage.

    Let us consider in more detail what 2 Kgs 17.24-33 says. It is true, we are told, that when the new peoples first settled in the land of Israel, they did not worship the LORD. When the lions, struck, however, they realised that the god of the land was against them, and they contacted the king of Assyria. He sent one of the exiled Israelite priests to Bethel, who taught them how to worship the LORD. The LORD was thus truly worshipped alongside all the various other gods of the peoples concerned. Merely to state what the passage is claiming is to see how at variance it is with the whole thrust of the story of Kings thus far. Its fundamental assumption is that the LORD is simply a local god. He must be appeased, certainly, by the new residents in his land. He must be worshipped correctly alongside all their other gods. But that is as far as their duty in matters of religion goes.

Now this is clearly at variance with what the remainder of Kings has to say about God and humankind. The God of whom the remainder of Kings knows is the LORD of all peoples and all history. He does sometimes use lions as his emissaries (1 Kgs 13.24-25; 20.35-36); but he is not confined to a single territory, and his demands are not limited in their scope. As the only God who exists, he claims exclusive worship. Those who point out the tension between 2 Kgs 17.29-33 and the remainder of the book are clearly quite justified. It is certainly unlikely that the author(s) of Kings who have told us all that has gone before should now seriously be telling us that a broad pantheon of gods is acceptable—that this new use of the high places, with its new priesthood (vv. 29, 32; cf. 1 Kgs 13.33), is any less reprehensible than the old Jeroboam cult which it has replaced. The kind of worship of the LORD which is taught by the exiled Israelite priest is evidently—and predictably, since the priest concerned bases himself in Bethel (cf. 1 Kgs 12.25–13.34)—just as flawed, from this point of view, as the worship which led to Israel's exile in the first place. And this is what 17.34-40 in fact tells us. So even if a 'source' is included here which spoke in polytheistic terms (that is, 17.24-33), it is presumably not included with the intention that we should take its various statements about religion at face value.

If it is unlikely, however, that the author(s) of Kings could have inserted such a passage intending their readers to take its 'voice' seriously, it is scarcely any more likely that a later editor would have done so. To imagine that this is the case, we must imagine an editor who either added all of 17.24-41, even though verses 34-40 undermined his own perspective (that it is possible simultaneously to fear the LORD and worship images), or simply added verse 41 to an already existing passage. In either case we have to reckon with an editor who wished to introduce a perspective to Kings radically at odds with the book as a whole, yet did so in an extraordinarily muted way, leaving the book as a whole apparently untouched. Such a person may well have existed; but the distinction between an almost invisible redactor and an entirely non-existent one is a fine one.

In fact we need not posit his existence at all. All that we need do to explain 2 Kgs 17.24-41 is to posit the presence of irony. The statements about religion in verses 24-33 and 41 are not meant to be taken at face value. The author(s) are simply setting up a particular point of view in order to demolish it—rather in the manner of a participant in a debating competition. That is the extent to which the 'voices' of 17.24-41 truly 'compete'. The tone of the passage is best caught, in fact, if the reader mentally supplies quotation marks to the words 'fear' and 'feared' in the RSV translation of verses 28 and 32-33. For the author of Kings certainly does not regard the 'worship' described in these verses as *true* worship—as vv. 34-39 make clear. It is an intrinsic feature of *true* worship, these verses tell us, that it is also *exclusive* worship. Any worship which is mixed is not truly worship of the living God at all; for he is a God who has from the beginning demanded 'You shall not fear other gods' (vv. 35, 37-38). What is clear by the end of the chapter on this view, then, is that the exile of Israel for her sins has not led to any improvement in the religion of the people dwelling in the land. They pursue their path of 'fearing' the LORD while serving their idols. Nothing has changed.

Our second example is the case of repetition in 2 Kgs 17.1-6 and 2 Kgs 18.9-12. Are we bound to see this repetition simply in terms of the rather unthinking duplication of information due to the combination of differing sources (e.g. Gray, 1977: 671-72)? Or is it possible to explain this, too, in terms of the conscious narrative art of a single author? The context in which the 'repetition' occurs may well be our best clue to its possible purpose. We have read in 2 Kgs 17.1-6 of a king whose name promised much (Hoshea, deriving from the Hebrew verb *yšʿ*, 'to save'), standing as he does in a long line of those through whom the LORD has brought salvation to Israel (Elisha, whose name is derived from the same verb; Jeroboam, 2 Kgs 14.27; other unnamed saviours, 2 Kgs 13.5). Hoshea is, indeed, a relatively good king as kings of Israel go (2 Kgs 17.2). Yet Israel is nevertheless taken into exile by the king of Assyria. Now in 2 Kings 18 we read of the best of the Judean kings so far: Hezekiah, whose trust in the LORD was unparalleled (v. 5). Here was a king who engaged in wholesale religious reform (vv. 3-6) and would not continue to serve the king of Assyria (v. 7). 2 Kings 18.9-12 function to remind us, to emphasize indeed, the kind of environment in which Hezekiah pursues this bold policy, and to prepare us for the story to come in 18.13–19.37. This was a time when rebellion against Assyria met with an aggressive, devastating response (vv. 9-11). We can hardly doubt that in such an environment, Judah, too, will soon be attacked. What will be the outcome then? The reminder in v. 12 that the people of the north, unlike the people of Judah under Hezekiah, had departed from 'all that Moses...commanded' (cf. 2 Kgs 17.7-23), is suggestive of a different fate for Judah, whose king clearly kept these same commands (v. 6). The Assyrian victory over the north was itself only possible because it was the will of God that Assyria should execute judgment on a sinful people. Yet it was under the best of the northern kings that judgment fell (2 Kgs 17.2). Is it possible that Hezekiah's reforms have come too late to make any difference? 2 Kgs 18.9-12 imply this question, and thus create narrative suspense. They may or may not derive from a different source from 17.1-6; but whether they do or not, they do not appear to be without purpose in their present location.

Our final example concerned the apparent differences in style and language between the regnal formulae in the majority of the book of Kings and those in the closing chapters. Does the 'rigidity' of these formulae necessarily imply that an original author of Kings has been imitated by one who lacked his creative flair? The problem with the argu-

ment is that this same 'rigidity' is found elsewhere in Kings.
As Nelson himself notes, the formulae for northern Israel's
kings also rigidify into a more static pattern towards the end
of that kingdom's history (1981: 33; cf. 2 Kgs 13.10; 14.24;
15.8, 18, 24, 28). Yet on this occasion, he offers a *literary*
explanation, rather than a redactional one. Hammering repetition, he affirms, expresses the stubbornness of the disobedience. Why is it that variations in the style and language of
the northern formulae are due to the creativity of a single
author, yet variations in the style and language of the south-
ern formulae necessitate that we posit a redactor? It is by no
means clear. What this example does indicate, however, is
just how subjective arguments from style and language can
be. The fact is that individual authors can and do vary their
style and language for their own particular literary purposes.

d. *The Story and the Larger Tale*
A review of the data that I presented earlier as examples of
'incoherence' in Kings has demonstrated that we are by no
means compelled to the conclusion, at least in these three
examples, that incoherence does in fact exist. The working
hypothesis that Kings may be read as a unified whole has
proved plausible in these cases. In the nature of the case,
that is as far as we may go in a brief guide to the book. This
is not a commentary. My own view, however, is that our
findings in these cases are entirely in line with what we find
elsewhere in Kings when we approach traditional modern
readings of the book in the same spirit of critical enquiry.
When a different set of general expectations is brought to the
text as narrative, accompanied by a willingness to give careful attention to individual passages in their broader and nar-
rower contexts within the book as a whole, difficulties with
regard to the unity of Kings tend to evaporate in a cloud of
admiration for the artistry and skill with which the text has
been constructed.

  This does not necessarily imply, of course, that the book of
Kings was after all produced by a single author at one particular moment in time, never to be touched by human hand
again. It is possible to conceive of a text which is artistically
and skilfully constructed, yet the product nevertheless of a

number of authors/editors working over an extended period of time. There are reasons other than 'tensions' in the text which might lead us to such a conclusion in respect of a particular text. In fact, I do believe that good reasons exist in the case of Kings to believe that it was not produced at one time by a single hand. I am persuaded, in fact, that the books of the Old Testament generally grew gradually into their present form in dialogue with each other, each shaping the developing tradition and being shaped by it. Only thus is it possible to explain the high level of what we may term 'intertextuality' in the Old Testament—the way in which individual books either share portions of text with other books, or quote them, or otherwise reveal that they are aware of them (e.g. by narrating stories in such a manner that they evoke other stories with which they might usefully be compared or contrasted—what I shall refer to as 'narrative patterning'). The degree of intertextuality within the Old Testament has often been underestimated, largely because modern scholars working on individual Old Testament books have seen their main task as interpreting the reconstructed 'original text' of the individual book in relation to its presumed historical context, rather than as interpreting it, as it is, in its larger literary context. Yet it is a marked feature of our Old Testament texts, and one which implies an extended history of composition in which it was possible for mutual influence to take place.

So far as the book of Kings is concerned, for instance, we may note first of all the large sections of text which are essentially shared with the books of Isaiah and Jeremiah. 2 Kgs 18.17–20.19 bears striking similarity to Isaiah 36.1–38.8; 38.21–39.8; while 2 Kgs 24.18–25.30 parallels Jer. 52.1-34. Secondly, at a lower level of sharing, but not therefore less significant, we may observe the way in which the closing words of the prophet Micaiah in 1 Kgs 22.28 are also the opening words of the prophet Micah in Micah 1.2. At the very least we are thus invited to consider the book of Micah and the story in 1 Kings 22 in relation to each other. The former is, indeed, an interesting book to read against the background of the whole Ahab story, looking forward as it does to the destruction of Samaria because of idolatry and prostitution (1.2-7) and condemning both social injustice (2.1-5) and false prophecy (2.6-11; 3.1-12). The Solomon story, likewise, frequently echoes themes from the book of Proverbs, as it grapples with the nature and consequences of that king's 'wisdom'.

Finally, we may consider a particular example of 'narrative patterning' in 1 Kings 12, where Jeroboam king of Israel is first of all presented as a Moses figure, leading his people out from slavery under the house of 'Pharaoh' (Rehoboam), only to be transformed later into an Aaron figure who fashions golden calves for them to worship. The people's complaint as the chapter opens is that they are no longer the people set free to live in the promised land. They have become once more a people under harsh labour, as they were in Egypt (Exod. 1.14; 2.23), toiling as oxen would under a heavy yoke. Jeroboam's similarity to Moses in this situation extends in the Hebrew (cf. the RSV footnote to v. 2) to a certain reluctance to take on such a role (cf. Exod. 4.1-17). He remains in Egypt, we are told, and has to be sent for. Rehoboam takes a hard line in response to these complaints (1 Kgs 12.8-11), behaving exactly as Pharaoh had behaved before him by increasing the oppression (cf. Exod. 5.1-21). It is divinely ordained so (v. 15): in the midst of all the human decisions, God's decision is being carried through. Echoes of the hardening of Pharaoh's heart (Exod. 4.21; 7.3-4, 13; and so on) are distinctly audible. No sooner has the new Exodus taken place, however, than it leads (as the first had done) to sin—to the worship of golden calves. Jeroboam, like Aaron (Exod. 32.1-35), makes gods for the people to worship in defiance of the LORD's words at Mount Sinai (Exod. 20.4). His words to them in 1 Kings 12.28 ('Here are your gods, O Israel, who brought you up out of Egypt') are, indeed, almost exactly the words with which the people greet the construction of the first calf (Exod. 32.4). His subsequent actions also recall Aaron. For Aaron, too, having made his golden calf, built an altar and announced a festival on a date of his own choosing (cf. Exod. 32.5); and it was the Levites who on that occasion also were to be found distanced from the celebrations (Exod. 32.26).

The story is told in such a manner that its evokes other

stories with which it might usefully be compared or contrasted. This is not an isolated instance, but a recurring feature of the book of Kings. The kings of Judah are compared
and contrasted with David; Elijah recalls Moses; both
Manasseh and Josiah, in their own ways, remind us of Ahab;
and so on. It is all part of the way in which the story is integrated into the larger tale.

It is this kind of evidence which suggests that the book of
Kings is intrinsically bound up, not only with the other books
of the 'Deuteronomistic History' which it so obviously presup-
poses, but also with that much wider circle of literature
which was to develop into what is known as Tanak by Jews
and the Old Testament by Christians. It suggests that Kings
grew gradually into its present form in dialogue with other
Old Testament books, shaping the developing tradition and
being shaped by it. It was not the product of a single author
in a particular place at a particular moment in time. For this
reason I shall from this point on use the plural 'authors'
when referring to the composition of the book.

Further Reading

For a brief and accessible introduction to the general issues raised in this
    chapter:
T. Longman III, *Literary Approaches to Biblical Interpretation* (FCI; Grand
    Rapids: Academie Books, 1987).

Essential reading for those interested in the composition of Kings remains:
M. Noth, *The Deuteronomistic History* (JSOTSup, 15; Sheffield: JSOT Press,
    1981), an English translation of the 1943 German original.

For summaries of the main positions with regard to composition and editing:
I.W. Provan, *Hezekiah and the Books of Kings: A Contribution to the Debate
    about the Composition of the Deuteronomistic History* (BZAW, 172;
    Berlin: De Gruyter, 1988), pp. 1-31.
S.L. McKenzie, *The Trouble with Kings: The Composition of the Book of
    Kings in the Deuteronomistic History* (VTSup, 42; Leiden: Brill, 1991),
    pp. 1-19.

For a helpful discussion of the sources which are often thought to lie behind
    the book:
G.H. Jones, *1 and 2 Kings* (NCB; 2 vols.; Grand Rapids: Eerdmans, 1984), I,
    pp. 47-77.

On the diversity of style and language in the regnal formulae:
R.D. Nelson, *The Double Redaction of the Deuteronomistic History* (JSOTSup, 18; Sheffield: JSOT Press, 1981).

For discussion of such compositional issues in the context of ancient history-writing:
B.O. Long, *1 Kings, with an Introduction to Historical Literature* (FOTL; Grand Rapids; Eerdmans, 1984), pp. 14-21. A brief introduction.
J. Van Seters, *In Search of History: Historiography in the Ancient World and the Origins of Biblical History* (New Haven: Yale University Press, 1983). An extensive treatment.

On Hebrew narrative in general:
R. Alter, *The Art of Biblical Narrative* (London: Allen & Unwin, 1981).
S. Bar-Efrat, *Narrative Art in the Bible* (Sheffield: Almond Press, 1989).
A. Berlin, *Poetics and Interpretation of Biblical Narrative* (Sheffield: Almond Press, 1983).
D.M. Gunn and D.N. Fewell, *Narrative in the Hebrew Bible* (OBS; Oxford: Oxford University Press, 1993).
J. Licht, *Storytelling in the Bible* (Jerusalem: Magnes Press, 1978).
M. Sternberg, *The Poetics of Biblical Narrative: Ideological Literature and the Drama of Reading* (Bloomington: Indiana University Press, 1985).

On intertextuality within the Old Testament in particular:
D.A. Carson and H.G.M. Williamson (eds.), *It Is Written: Scripture Citing Scripture. Essays in Honour of Barnabas Lindars* (Cambridge: Cambridge University Press, 1988), pp. 25-83.
M. Fishbane, *Biblical Interpretation in Ancient Israel* (Oxford: Clarendon Press, 1985).

Commentaries which take a keen interest in reading Kings in its present form as narrative:
T.R. Hobbs, *2 Kings* (WBC; Waco, TX: Word Books, 1985)—see especially his excellent introduction 'On Reading 2 Kings', pp. xxvi-xxx.
B.O. Long, *1 Kings, and 2 Kings* (FOTL; Grand Rapids; Eerdmans, 1984, 1991).
R.D. Nelson, *First and Second Kings* (IBC; Louisville: John Knox, 1987).
I.W. Provan, *1 and 2 Kings* (NIBC; Peabody, MA: Hendrickson; Carlisle: Paternoster, 1995).

3

THE BOOK OF KINGS
AS HISTORIOGRAPHICAL LITERATURE

In certain respects it would be accurate to describe the attention recently given to the biblical narrative texts as literature simply in terms of a redressing of the balance. If in the modern period there has been a tendency to view the text as a quarry out of which 'facts' may be mined—a tendency to look behind the text rather than at it—now we find an insistence that the text should be taken seriously as story. When the pendulum begins to swing in trends of thought, however, balance is not always the outcome. Reaction can bring about an imbalance of a quite different kind at the opposite end of the intellectual spectrum.

This is certainly the case with much of the recent work on biblical narrative. What is striking about much of this work is the marked reluctance of the authors concerned, in affirming the importance of reading the biblical text as story, also to affirm the importance of dealing with it as an account of the past. It is acknowledged that a book like Kings gives the impression of speaking about the past. It is conceded that a history-like element is an obvious and important feature of this kind of book. Emphasis is laid upon the life-likeness of much of the depiction, the lack of artificiality or heroic elevation in so much of the story. This is 'realistic narrative'. Yet there is at the same time a greater or lesser degree of resistance to the idea that the world which is thus portrayed has anything to do with the 'real' world of the past. It is a narrative world, a 'fictive world', entire in itself and referring only to itself. Its integrity must not be compromised by seeking to relate it to anything outside itself. Text and history must be kept apart. In all of this we see a strong reaction against the kind of historical reading of the biblical texts which, so far as many recent writers are concerned, has succeeded only in rendering books like Kings unreadable, as scholars have battled over the bits and pieces while obscuring the whole. The response of these writers to what they view as literary Philistinism is to pursue a policy of aggressive exclusion, by affirming that the sort of historical questions which other scholars have characteristically asked of the text are simply irrelevant. It does not matter whether what Kings says corresponds to what appears to have happened in historical Israel. All that matters is that the story makes sense in itself, and when read along with other Old Testament stories.

The interesting thing about this attempt by literary critics to create a secure zone in which biblical texts can be enjoyed as literature and awkward questions about historical reference can be avoided is that increasingly little opposition to it is being voiced by those with historical interests in the Old Testament period. It is not only those with literary interests who wish to keep text and history apart. It is increasingly the historians themselves. It has become fashionable among some historians of Israel, in fact, to distinguish quite self-consciously between 'biblical Israel' and 'historical Israel'. 'Historical Israel' is the real Israel which occupied the central Palestinian highlands for just over two centuries and has left its traces in Palestinian soil. This Israel is to be studied by looking at the artifacts which were left by its people, the buildings which they occupied, and the literature which they certainly wrote (that is, datable inscriptions), all within the framework of general theory about such things as social and state formation. 'Biblical Israel', on the other hand—the Israel presented to us in the Old Testament—is a literary construct. It is a picture of Israel which has some points of contact with the past, but which is so ideologically slanted, so biased in its outlook, that it cannot serve as the starting-point for serious historical enquiry. It must be set aside, as we attempt to replace fiction with facts—as a truly critical scholarship takes over from a scholarship which has been compromised by religious sentiment, and which has therefore accepted too easily what the text has to say.

A form of apartheid has increasingly become popular, then, on all sides. Some like it because it offers the prospect of insulating both text and reader against the chilly winds of historical enquiry. Others favour it because it clears the way for the progress of *proper* historical enquiry, as the last demons of religious presupposition are forever exorcised from the scholarly community. It is not a sufficient response to this situation, although it must be an important part of any response, to argue that a book like Kings clearly has historiographical intent and that to fail to take this seriously is to fail to take the book seriously—a failure as profound as the failure to read the book as a book. A full response requires further reflection on the nature of historiography itself.

1. The Nature of Historiography

It is a pronounced feature of much of the recent writing on the history of Israel that it is working implicitly or explicitly with a particular kind of model of the historian's task which makes it difficult to take a book like Kings very seriously as historiography, whatever might be construed as the claims of the text about its own nature. The historian, on this model, is a scientist, labouring to distinguish what we know from what we do not know, to distinguish reality from unreality; anxious to avoid speculation and mere prejudice, and to arrive at the objective truth. His task is to describe 'what happened', in a manner similar to that of physical scientists whose task might be thought of as describing 'what is there'. It stands to reason that if this is how the task of the historian is understood, a book like Kings will not be highly regarded as history-writing; for art, particularly ideologically motivated art, has no place in the world of this 'historian-understood-as-scientist'. Science and art are different things; and literature of the biblical sort falls on the wrong side of the ditch dug between them.

Whether we should accept the general notion of science which lies at the root of this view of history-writing is, of course, open to question, even if it happens to be very much the notion that inhabits the popular imagination. Philosophers of science realize all too well just how problematic the idea of 'objective scientific truth' really is: how what is perceived in the so-called 'real' world is always and inevitably connected with the knowledge, the prejudices, the ideologies which the person doing the perceiving brings with him or her. They have described clearly the ways in which the great broad theories of science are under-determined by the facts, and even of how experiments are themselves, from the moment of their conception, shaped by the theories of those conducting them. They have shown how the myth of the neutral, uninvolved observer has functioned and continues to function as an ideological tool in the hands of those whose political and economic interests it has served. Scientific theories, they have argued, come and go, partly on the basis of their success in prediction and control of the environment, but partly also on the basis of the interests which they serve in a particular culture, be they theological and metaphysical, sociological or simply aesthetic. Scientists cannot, any more than other human beings, escape from this matter of 'interests'. There is no such thing as value-free academic endeavour.

If this is true of science in general, it is certainly true of 'history-as-science' in particular. The suggestion that there are hard facts which simply 'exist', the bedrock upon which the historian can build his or her 'objective' picture of the past; the suggestion that any historian might observe and describe the past without indulging in theorizing and hypothesizing and philosophizing—such suggestions cannot and should not be taken seriously. The reality is that every time one offers an explanation of a piece of pottery in the ground; every time one correlates an ancient inscription with other information from an archaeological site; every time one makes a connection between population movements and climatic conditions; on every such occasion, one is theorizing and hypothesizing, assessing probability, and using analogy and guesswork. There can be no attempt at understanding the past which does not involve these things. There is no history-writing without them. And in the process of doing all these things, one is inevitably bringing one's own worldview to bear, in terms of fundamental beliefs and prejudices, in terms of ideology. Most importantly from our present perspective, one is inevitably *telling a story* (cf. Davies 1992: 13-14, on this point). Historiography is story: it is narrative about the past. Historiography is also ideological literature: narrative about the past which involves, among other things, the selection of material and its interpretation by authors who are intent on persuading themselves and their readership in some way. It is a narrative, moreover, which is under-determined by the facts in precisely the same way that each broad scientific theory is under-determined by the facts. All historiography is like this, whether ancient, or mediaeval, or modern; whether we are thinking of the anonymous authors of ancient conquest accounts; of Thucydides or of Bede; of Gibbon, or Macaulay, or Michelet; or whether we are thinking, indeed, of the works of the modern historians of ancient Israel, all of whom tell a story so that we who hear it may believe. Science and art cannot be so simplistically divorced as they often have been in modern thinking about historiography. The reality is that they are very much bound up with each other.

2. Biblical Narrative and Historiography

If all narrative about the past has this story-like quality about it, however, then why is it that such a gulf has been fixed between history and story in so much of the recent reflection on the *biblical* narratives about *Israel's* past? Why is the nature of these *particular* narratives as story thought to be so problematic? And why, conversely, is history reckoned to be found more 'objectively' in other kinds of data, such as those collected from archaeological digs? It is often difficult, in truth, to follow the logic of the arguments at this point.

Ahlström, for example, is apparently ready to concede in some of his writing (e.g. Ahlström 1993: 22-23, 31) the necessity of the subjective involvement of the historian, with all his or her own particular philosophical presuppositions, in the construction of history. He is prepared to concede the inevitability of such involvement in the face of archaeological material which is, as he puts it, 'mute'. Yet elsewhere (Ahlström 1991: 117, 120) the same author does write of archaeological remains speaking for themselves, rather than through the Bible, and says:

> If the meaning of the archaeological evidence is clear, one might say that it gives a more 'neutral' history than the textual material. It is free from the *Tendenz* or evaluation that easily creeps into an author's writings.

Mute data have suddenly found a voice: a value-free, neutral voice, which can be trusted. For Ahlström, the stories which archaeologists tell can apparently be trusted to inform us directly about reality, to reveal to us 'the facts'. The biblical stories, conversely, often contain description which is ideological, rather than factual. Much of what was written down was carefully selected by writers more concerned to promote their own viewpoint than with historical truth. It is consequently not clear how the biblical texts relate to what history really looked like; and thus the archaeology of Palestine, rather than the biblical texts, must become the main source for historiography in respect of Israel (cf. Ahlström 1993: 28-29, 36, 42, 50).

None of this makes much sense. The concept of 'what history really looked like', first of all, is logically incoherent, as the simple question 'looked like to whom'? illustrates. Disinterested objectivity of the sort apparently envisaged by Ahlström is quite impossible, whether in ancient historiographers or modern; the uninvolved, disinterested observer has never existed. Secondly, selectivity cannot be traded off quite so simplistically against historical truth without calling in question, not just biblical historiography, but all historiography; for all historiography is selective. It is also the case, thirdly, that all historiography—including Ahlström's own book—is ideological in nature (see above). So what is it that is fundamentally problematic about biblical narrative as historiography, when compared with modern efforts to write about the past? Ahlström's work, at least, does not appear to provide us with any satisfactory answer to the question.

Nor is the answer found in the other books and articles of recent years which adopt a similar line. If one is prepared to question either the coherence of the notion of 'what history really looked like'; or the affirmation that modern historians of all mortal beings on earth are in a position to perceive 'what really happened' accurately and to form 'unprejudiced' opinions about it; or the curious idea (e.g. Smelik 1992: 11-15, 23) that 'real' historiography is the sort that one finds in annals, rather than the sort one finds in narratives; then most of the case presented collapses. It remains only to tie up the few loose ends represented by arguments from the presumed lateness of the biblical narratives in their present form.

Thompson, for example, believes that the biblical traditions became a relatively coherent whole only late on in Israelite history (the Persian period), when they were provided with their literary frameworks. He argues that this makes it difficult to affirm the historicity of the Israel of tradition at all (Thompson 1992: 82, 353-57). We may leave aside here the question of whether there is, in fact, as much 'incoherence' in Hebrew narrative as Thompson seems to presuppose, referring the reader back to the discussion of narrative in chapter 2. We may also leave aside the issue of whether Thompson is correct in his general views about the dating of Old Testament texts, which would certainly be disputed by many. What we must particularly question here is the assumption that 'historicality' is somehow tied up with what is 'primary' rather than what is 'secondary' and 'late'. On the one hand, eyewitnesses, like everyone else, have a point of view. On the other hand, the historian who writes at distance from the events he or she describes may be in a better position than the eyewitness to describe them, and particularly to reveal the larger patterns, structures and meanings behind particular events and facts which contemporaries were not able to see. What is 'secondary' may well be *different* from what is 'primary;' but one cannot argue logically from the mere *distance* of a text from the events it describes directly to its *usefulness* as historiography or otherwise. It is remarkable that modern writers with aspirations to be regarded as historians (rather than, say, novelists) should in any case wish to employ such an argument in such a way, given their own vulnerable location twenty-five hundred years or more distant from the events they seek to describe.

One can only imagine that they do not fully appreciate its nature as an extremely sharp double-edged sword.

Our conclusion must be this: that there is nothing about the nature of the biblical narratives like Kings as story which makes them *particularly* problematic when it comes to reading them also as historiography. The suggestion that this is so arises from a misunderstanding about what historiography in general is. It is this misunderstanding which has in turn bred the selective scepticism which is so evident among many of the recent historians of Israel. The biblical stories about Israel, on the one hand, are approached with the maximum degree of suspicion in regard to the extent to which they truly reflect the past. There is, on the other hand, a touching degree of (sometimes quite uncritical) faith displayed when it comes to modern narratives about this same entity (written by archaeologists, anthropologists, and so on). The attitude is as unjustified as the misunderstanding is unfortunate. The interweaving of history and story is a feature of every narrative about the past, and confronts all those who read such narratives. Those who understand this general truth will be much more careful than many recent writers have found themselves able to be in what they say about *biblical* narrative concerning the past in particular.

3. The Book of Kings and the History of Israel

The current state of the discipline of Old Testament studies has necessitated something of an extended digression from the particular concern of this guide, which is to introduce readers to the book of Kings. We are now in a better position, however, to take up this task once again, as we turn to consider the book in its nature as historiography.

We may immediately grant that the picture of Israel which is contained in the book of Kings is only *one* portrait of the past among the many which it might have been possible to paint. It is an implication of everything stated above that it could not be otherwise. The book of Kings, to the extent that it is indeed a coherent work (see Chapter 2), cannot do more than give us a particular account of the history of Israel from a particular point of view. I used the word 'portrait' above quite deliberately because it communicates well the reality upon which I have already touched several times: that historiography is art, and not science (in what we may now call the old-fashioned and outdated sense of the latter term). It may be more fully described, in fact, as a kind of a verbal representational art, analogous to the visual type of representational art which is known as 'painting'. To think of historiography in this way is helpful in a context where we are having to address the question of how an artistically constructed story can nevertheless be understood as reflecting an external reality. For the painting of a garden scene, for example, can be very much a representation of reality, imparting to receptive viewers a true sense and appreciation of the scene, while at the same time being a 'fictional' rather than a 'literal' rendering of reality, in the sense that there is no question of the artist counting blades of grass or leaves on trees. Art and representation do not necessarily have to be thought of as in competition, even where the artist may use techniques which are at one level indistinguishable from those employed by abstract or expressionist painters whose aims are quite different from his own.

a. *Selection and Proportion*

The book of Kings is only one portrait of Israel's past among the many which it might have been possible to paint. It is, in the first place, a highly selective account. Its authors never pretend otherwise. The regnal formulae continually point us to sources from which, it is implied, the material in Kings has been drawn (e.g. 1 Kgs 11.41; 14.19, 29), thus making it quite explicit that a substantial amount of material which the authors knew has been omitted. When we turn to the remainder of the book, it is quite clear that we are not informed there of everything that happened in the region of Palestine during that part of the Iron Age about which the authors are writing. Extra-biblical texts claim, for example, that Assyrian kings had been campaigning in the west long before Menachem of Israel's reign, which is described for us in 2 Kgs 15.17-22. It is, however, in 2 Kgs 15.17-22 that Assyria is first mentioned by the authors of Kings. Even after this point, Assyria is referred to in Kings relatively infrequently—mainly in the story of the siege of Jerusalem in

2 Kgs 15.18-19 (cf. also 20.6), otherwise only in 2 Kgs 15.29; 16.7-10, 18; 17.3-6, 23-27; 23.29. In other words, Assyria plays only a minor part in the overall drama of 2 Kgs 15–23. Yet according to extra-biblical texts again, Assyria was engaging in quite a bit of activity 'off-stage' throughout this period. The authors of Kings have selected only those incidents which serve their own purposes in narrating Israel's story.

It is not simply what is selected, however, which is influenced by this overall purpose; it is also the amount of space afforded to what is selected. It is a striking feature of the book that fairly long periods of time can be passed over relatively briefly, while periods of a year or less can be described at great length. We may note, for instance, that whereas the account of Manasseh's reign of fifty-five years occupies only eighteen verses (2 Kgs 21.1-18), the account of the religious reform in Josiah's eighteenth year takes up forty-one (2 Kgs 22.3–23.23). Zimri, who ruled for seven days (1 Kgs 16.15-20), gets almost as much space as Omri (1 Kgs 16.21-28), who ruled for twelve years, and Azariah (2 Kgs 15.1-7), who ruled for fifty-two. Some of this may simply be a consequence of the differing extent of the information available to the authors. Yet this is unlikely to be the entire explanation. It is almost certainly the case that, for example, the prominence of Josiah's reform is to be explained in terms of its importance to the book as a whole, and that Manasseh is given just sufficient space to establish him as Josiah's opposite—the worst Judean royal sinner of all, whose other achievements (alluded to in 2 Kgs 21.17) were irrelevant to the task in hand. Omri is a particularly interesting case when considering the question of relevance, for he appears in Assyrian records as an important political figure of some weight. If the authors of Kings had evidence to suggest the same, they have not passed it on. To them, Omri was scarcely more important than his unfortunate predecessor Zimri. Both came to the throne, sinned and died. That was virtually all that needed to be said.

b. *The Religious and the 'Secular'*
It is already clear that what is driving this particular representation of Israel's past is a religious concern. The authors are not particularly interested in what modern readers might

call 'political history', if by that is meant a politics which is relatively independent of religion. In this book politics and religion are intertwined; and even where we are given information which at first sight may appear to be more 'political' than 'religious', closer inspection suggests that in fact this information is itself very much tied up with the religious perspective of the whole book. Thus we are sometimes told of various achievements or failures of Judean kings in language which appears 'neutral', as if the authors had suddenly come across something in their sources which they thought interesting, but of no particular religious significance. We are told of Asa's war with Baasha, for example (1 Kgs 15.16-22); and this kind of information has often been regarded as more 'secular' than much of what we find elsewhere in the book. The fact is, however, that Asa's reign (like those of other Judaean kings) is patterned on the earlier reign of Solomon and is meant to be read in that context.

Asa is presented as a good king (1 Kgs 15.11-15), rather like the early Solomon. He eschewed idolatry and brought into the temple of the LORD the silver and gold and the articles that he and his father had dedicated (cf. 1 Kgs 7.51), yet unwisely failed to intervene to end worship at the local sanctuaries or 'high places' (cf. 1 Kgs 3.2-3). The story in 1 Kgs 15.16-22 draws further parallels between the two kings. For all that Asa was like the early Solomon, he knew no peace of the kind that Solomon knew. There was war between Asa and Baasha, king of Israel, throughout their reigns (15.16, repeated for emphasis in 15.32). So precarious was Asa's position, indeed, as Baasha pushed into Benjamin and fortified Ramah, only a few miles north of Jerusalem, that far from treasures flowing into the city from places like Aram, Asa was forced to send a substantial gift north to Damascus to try to buy a new friend (vv. 18-19). This was a 'wise' thing to do (Prov. 17.8). Yet one cannot help but notice that whereas Solomon had the upper hand in his treaty with Hiram (1 Kgs 5; 9.10-14), Asa is quite clearly the suppliant in regard to Ben-Hadad. He does not even receive any help with the stones and timber for the building work which results from the treaty (v. 22; cf. 5.18). He has to resort to the imposition of forced labour upon his Judean citizens. Nor can it escape our attention that whereas Solomon's political arrangements contributed to the maintenance of the empire, Asa's strategy results in the loss of parts of Israel to a foreign king (v. 20). The point is that faithfulness like Solomon's no longer brings Solomon's glory in its wake. These are different times—times of humbling for David's descendants (11.39).

Even apparently 'secular' material, then, is not included in Kings without having some significance in relation to the overall religious purpose of the book. The telling of the history is dominated by the religious convictions of the authors. These convictions are, moreover, those of a particular group within the Israelite community, rather than those of the whole community. This is clear from the book itself. Even the relatively good kings who are presented to us, with the exception of Hezekiah and Josiah, fail to live up to the highest ideals of the authors of the book: they fail to remove the high places (cf. 1 Kgs 3.2-3; 22.43 [MT 22.44]; 2 Kgs 12.3; 14.4; 15.4, 35). Some Judean kings are much worse: they lead their people into idolatry of one kind or another (cf., e.g., 2 Kgs 8.16-19, 25-27). The people of the northern kingdom are presented as living in a constant state of apostasy from the LORD, whether it is simply that they participate in the worship instituted by Jeroboam (cf., e.g., 1 Kgs 12.25-33; 2 Kgs 17.21-23) or that they become devotees of Baal and Asherah (cf., e.g., 1 Kgs 16.29-33; 2 Kgs 10.18-29). It is clear, then, that we cannot straightforwardly identify the religious perspective from which the story of Kings is told with the religion of Israel as it was universally practised by Israelites. The book itself suggests that attempts to put into practice the requirements of 'the book of the Law' which appears so prominently in 2 Kings 22–23 were sporadic and partial at best, and that for much of the period of the monarchy the actual religion of Israel was far from what the authors would have wished to see. There is, however, much more to be said about the religion of Israel than this. The matter upon which we are touching here is a large one, which will require extended treatment by itself in a separate chapter (see Chapter 4). I shall therefore not pursue it further here, but rather move straight to an extended example of the historiography found in Kings, which will enable us to explore in a more focused way some of the issues which have thus far have arisen in this chapter.

4. Extended Example:
The Assyrian Invasion of Judah (2 Kgs 18.13–19.37)

Accounts of the Assyrian invasion of Judah are not only found in 2 Kgs 18.13–19.37 and in a slightly different form in Isaiah 36–37, but also in the Assyrian records (cf. the Rassam Prism Inscription of the Assyrian king Sennacherib). We leave aside 2 Chron. 32.1-23 so as not to over-complicate the issue. The Kings account opens with a passage not found in the Isaiah parallel (18.13-16), which tells us of Hezekiah's initial unsuccessful attempt, after Sennacherib had taken 'all the fortified cities of Judah', to buy off the Assyrian king. Thereafter the two accounts proceed in tandem, telling of Hezekiah's refusal to surrender Jerusalem to the besieging Assyrians; his consultation with the prophet Isaiah and Isaiah's promise of deliverance for the city; his later prayer and Isaiah's response to that prayer; the eventual miraculous deliverance of Jerusalem through an angel, and Sennacherib's death. The Assyrian account, on the other hand, in those places where it concerns Judah in particular rather than Palestine in general, does not mention any initial payment by Hezekiah after the fall of his cities. It moves straight from description of their fall to description of the siege of Jerusalem. It does not explicitly tell us the circumstances in which the siege ended, although it implies that Hezekiah at this point did agree to pay tribute, which he is then described as sending to Assyria after Sennacherib had departed from Judah.

All three accounts of the passage of events described are, of course, bound to be 'ideological' in nature. The story must inevitably be told from a particular point of view and with a particular purpose. Broader consideration of Assyrian accounts like the one we have just described might suggest that its overall purpose is to exalt the reputation of the king concerned; to glorify the gods of Assyria, especially Ashur; and to encourage loyalty and submission among his subjects. This is certainly consistent with the fact that such accounts are not noted for the frank admission of failure, even where the readers of other, non-Assyrian texts might reasonably deduce that failure has occurred. As Younger has recently underlined (1990: 61-124), all these Assyrian royal inscriptions cater to preconceived ideological requirements in the way that they are structured. Their stereotypical nature instils in the readers a sense of anticipation of the obvious outcome of the campaign described, and hence of the relentless efficacy of the Assyrian king's actions as he seeks to reinstate (what is from the Assyrian point of view) order, righteousness and life.

Then again, the story in Kings clearly reflects the interests of those who produced the book. The account of the reign of wicked Ahaz in 2 Kings 16, together with the account of Israel's exile in 2 Kings 17, has raised serious questions about Judah's future. It seems that Judah, like Israel, may be heading for exile, unless she heeds the prophetic warnings she has received and turns away from her sins. It is at this point in the narrative that we are presented with Hezekiah, the 'second David' of the book of Kings who does what is right 'according to all that David his father had done', reforming Judean worship and making it what it should be (18.3-4). In at least one respect, in fact, there was no-one like him among all the kings of Judah—the way in which he trusted in the LORD (v. 5). By the same token he was utterly dissimilar to Ahaz, for he would not continue to serve the king of Assyria (cf. 2 Kgs 16.7), but rebelled against him. Foreign influence or domination, of whatever kind, is rejected. The focus of the narrative is thus upon what will happen when the king of Assyria attempts to take the kind of vengeance on Judah which he has just inflicted upon Israel.

The beginning is not promising. For all that Hezekiah has been lauded as a king quite unlike anyone who preceded him, his first response to foreign attack is not unfamiliar to readers of Kings. He deals with the crisis by raiding the temple of the LORD and the treasuries of the royal palace, even stripping the gold from the doors and doorposts of the temple (cf. 1 Kgs 15.18-19; 2 Kgs 12.17-18 [MT 12.18-19]; 16.7-8). We are presumably to regard this as a regrettable lapse; for the narrative then goes on to show Hezekiah in a much better light.

His 'trust' in the LORD is, indeed, the issue which lies at the heart of 2 Kgs 18.19-25 (cf. vv. 19, 20, 21, 22, 24) and of the remainder of the story. The Assyrian king presents himself through his messengers as an alternative deity (cf., e.g., 18.31-35, where he claims that the LORD cannot deliver Jerusalem because he is simply one of many powerless gods and offers himself in the LORD's place as the true provider of material blessings and life itself). Hezekiah, however, adheres to the truth that the God of Israel is not merely one god among many, but God alone, while the gods of the various nations are only wood and stone. His request that Jerusalem be delivered from the Assyrian's hand so that all the kingdoms on earth should know the difference between God and the gods is duly answered in the activity of the angel. The message is that faithfulness to the living God and his laws makes a difference to Israel's historical experience. Israel knows blessing in obedience, even in the face of overwhelming odds.

The story also has its own function within the book of Isaiah. Isaiah 36–39 function within the book as a counterpart to Isaiah 6.1–9.6, where a critique of the Davidic dynasty and the ruling king Ahaz (Isa. 7) is followed by the promise of a Davidic child (8.23–9.6) in whom the promises to David will be realized. This child to whom such great expectations attach is perhaps most naturally taken in the first instance to be Ahaz's son, Hezekiah (cf. Isa. 11.1-10; 14.28-32); and in Isaiah 36–39 his reign is duly described, in a way which appears to heighten his piety in relation to the book of Kings. An additional prayer is inserted (Isa. 38.9-20); and as we have seen, there is no mention of that rather questionable paying of tribute to the Assyrians. The positioning of Isaiah 36–39 immediately before the oracles of glorious deliverance and restoration which begin in Isaiah 40 is important. Isaiah 40–55 testify, within the book as a whole, to Israel's future with God; and the figure of Hezekiah himself is drawn into this vision of the nation's future by the structuring of the book which makes his reign so central to it. Isaiah 6.1–9.6 (with the other associated passages mentioned above) imply that Hezekiah is the 'second David' who is completely to fulfil God's promises: it is in his lifetime that the anticipated era of universal peace and security will be ushered in. Isaiah 36–39 also make this link between Hezekiah and God's promises. The impression is given by the immediate juxtaposition of Isaiah 39.8 ('There will be peace and security in my lifetime') with the beginning of the words of consolation in Isaiah 40 (and indeed the absence of any note of Hezekiah's death and burial, such as is found in this position in Kings) that the promises will indeed come to pass, in some sense, in 'Hezekiah's' reign. In other words, it seems that the figure of Hezekiah has himself become within the literary context of the book of Isaiah just as fully eschatological as Isaiah 40–55. Isaiah 8.23–9.6 themselves encourage this theological move, of course, because of their portrayal of the future king as one possessing divine attributes, ushering in the reign of God. The total effect of all these texts within the context of the book of Isaiah as a whole is thus to identify Hezekiah as a paradigmatic king in whose reign the promises were yet unfulfilled, and who thus points beyond himself to another Davidic monarch to come. The use of the story of the Assyrian invasion is bound up with this larger purpose.

There is no question, then, but that each of the accounts we have discussed must be regarded as 'ideological' in nature. Must any of them at the same time be regarded as 'unhistorical'? We may return at this point to one of the authors already mentioned above, Philip Davies, who takes the Assyrian invasion as a particular example in the course of his argument about the folly of looking for 'ancient Israel' (cf. Davies 1992: 32-36). Davies is prepared to allow that behind our extant accounts there does lie an historical reality. A vassal king of Judah rebelled against the king of Assyria, and the Assyrians in response devastated Judah, depriving Hezekiah of all his kingdom except Jerusalem. Jerusalem was not captured, but Hezekiah paid a large tribute, and afterwards remained a vassal of Assyria without the power of rebellion. This is 'what happened' in the history of Palestine. The biblical story, on the other hand, tells us of a victory by the God of Israel over the Assyrian king which left Judah ever after free of Assyrian control (for such control is never referred to again). Why this story is as it is can in the last analysis be explained, claims Davies, only if we recognize that it is not simply giving us a different version of an historical event, but is telling us a story of something that is not historical. The analogy which he offers here is that of Shakespeare's *Julius Caesar*, where things happen because of the play's own dramatic logic. Whatever any historical Brutus may or may not have done does not either explain the actions of Shakespeare's character of that name nor make this character into an historical figure.

What are we to make of this argument? Here I must refer the reader back to the general case outlined in 3.1–3.3, which provides the broader context for the particular comments that will be made here. We may note, first of all, in evaluating Davies' argument, precisely that confidence in the ability of the modern historian to describe 'what really happened' which was earlier criticized. Here we are told 'what happened' in that part of the history of Palestine which concerns the Assyrian invasion of Judah; and this is contrasted with what the biblical story has to tell us (and implicitly also with what the Assyrian story has to say). But where, we may ask, has this knowledge of 'what happened' come from? Closer attention to the argument reveals that it originates in what is described as a 'reasonable guess' (Davies 1992: 34). How we get in the course of a few lines from this 'reasonable guess' to the kind of solid 'what really happened' which may be contrasted with what the ancient texts say (1992: 34 again) is not clear. It is particularly unclear because the description of 'what happened' is itself based upon these same ancient texts. It is, in fact, a new story derived from the ancient stories, which takes on a mysterious solidity which they apparently lack for reasons which are not fully spelled out.

If we enquire a little further, however, we do find some explanation for the story that Davies has chosen as the 'reality' which underlies at least the biblical story in the following:

> The events are described as they are because Israel is involved. And to this Israel happen things that as an historian I do not accept happen in history here or anywhere else (1992: 35).

The reference is clearly to the idea of supernatural deliverance through 'the angel'. Here we find a good illustration of the general truth discussed above, which is that all historiography involves bringing one's own worldview to bear on the subject matter, in terms of fundamental beliefs and prejudices, and in terms of ideology. There is a particular philosophy, a particular worldview, which is informing Davies's thinking as historian at this point. The surface appeal of the quotation is to analogy, which is commonly regarded as a touchstone of proper historical method—the idea that harmony with the normal, customary or at least frequently attested events and conditions as we have experienced them is the distinguishing mark of reality for the events which critical scholarship can recognize as really having happened in the past. Followed through in a narrow sense, however, this is clearly too restrictive, for historians regularly accept the reality of events and practices that lie outside their own immediate experience. Yet it is not clear that widening the sense so that 'general human experience' is taken into account helps us much either. How do we ascertain, for example, what is in fact normal, usual, or frequently attested? And even if we could ascertain this, would it follow that what is not normal, usual, or frequently attested cannot have happened? Again, there appear to be events which historians would accept as having happened which do not conform to the criterion (e.g., the first climbing of Mount Everest or the first human landing on the moon). The fact is that analogy never operates in a vacuum. There is '...an intimate relation between analogy and its context or network of background beliefs' (Abraham, 1982: 105); and conclusions drawn from an application of the principle of analogy are only as valid as the background beliefs held by those drawing the conclusions. The principle of analogy, in other words, always has operated and always will operate within the wider context of the background beliefs and experience of the historian concerned. To claim, therefore, that it is 'as an historian' that one does not accept this or that claim about reality is to some extent to mislead or to be misled. Philosophy, and for that matter religion, are as much a part of the equation as history.

What is clear, then, is that Davies's 'what happened around 701 BCE in Palestine' is in truth merely one story alongside others, and certainly not any objective yardstick against which the ancient stories can be measured in terms of their historicality. The 'reasonable guess' has all sorts of presuppositions and prejudices bound up with it which must be taken account of and which are already dictating the way in which the modern story is told. However, even if one did find it difficult to believe (for example) in angels, one would still have to press the question as to whether one is driven quite to Davies's position overall. *Is* it really true that in the last analysis the biblical story can be explained only if we recognize that it is not giving us a different version of an historical event, but is telling us a story of something that is not historical? Many scholars who are not prepared to see angels as a quite 'historical' category have nevertheless been prepared to believe that it might indeed have been an unusual event at the gates of Jerusalem which at least in part led to the withdrawal of the Assyrian army from Judah. This includes some of those I have generally taken issue with above (e.g. Ahlström 1993: 713-14; Lemche 1988: 70). That the Assyrians do not mention such an event, which some have speculated might have been plague, would not be surprising in view of the nature of the Assyrian records. That the Greek historian Herodotus (2: 141) records an Egyptian story in which Egypt is saved by divine intervention from Sennacherib's army is interesting in terms of the general parallel. Whether one can move quite so easily from the presence of angels in the biblical text to the assertion of its general non-historicality on the question of the Assyrian withdrawal must therefore be open to question.

What are the grounds, then, for doubting that our biblical story is indeed 'a different version of an historical event'? Davies's assertion is that the biblical story tells us that Judah was ever after the 'event' free of Assyrian control, whereas the 'facts' were otherwise. How secure our grasp of 'the facts' is on this point, unless we simply take the Assyrian claims at face value, is an interesting question; but it is worth noting in any case, as Davies himself allows, that the biblical text does not actually say that Judah was ever after the 'event' free of Assyrian control. The absence of references to the Assyrians cannot of itself be taken to indicate that this is what is implied, in a text which is selective

in the first place about what it records, especially regarding
Assyria (see 3.3 above). It is, of course, the case that the
Kings account differs from the Assyrian account in what it
has to say about the timing and content of the tribute; and it
may well be the case here that we must make a decision
about how far what one or both accounts has to say on
this point has more to do with the overall purposes of the
texts than with the past which they describe (see, e.g.,
Younger 1990: 122-24, for some interesting comments on the
significance of material goods in the Assyrian texts). On the
other hand, it could be that Hezekiah did indeed both
attempt to buy Sennacherib off before the siege and provide
future security for himself after it was over. In either case,
one is making a decision here on a particular point. One is
not adopting a general attitude towards the text on the basis
of a simplistic contrast between 'ideology' and 'history'. That
the artistically constructed story which we find in 2 Kgs
18.13–19.37 (and in slightly different form in Isaiah) also
reflects an external, historical reality is not something which
the data in themselves generally compel us to question.

5. Conclusion

The preceding discussion underlines the extent to which it is
not simply data which determine conclusions about the manner in which biblical texts refer to the past, but also philoso-
phies, beliefs, prejudices, and the like. Perhaps the most
striking prejudice of much modern scholarship in this regard
is that which concerns its own objectivity in respect of the
past. It is this prejudice more than anything else which
results in the exaltation of modern portraits of the past, however tenuously grounded in testimony and evidence, over
portraits from an earlier era—in the conviction that modern
portraits of an event, simply by being modern, are thereby
intrinsically 'better', that is 'more historical'. It requires
only a slight critical distance from this scholarly emperor to
discern clearly enough the extent to which he is without
clothing.

Once this critical distance is attained, the nature of
much modern discussion of biblical texts like Kings and their

historiographical 'value' will be more clearly seen. It will be more evident, then, to the student just how obviously personal and subjective is each modern scholarly rendering of the past, as artists paint the portrait which is right in their own eyes, according to various (and extremely varied) notions about what is 'probable', and 'possible', and so on, and according to how far biblical and others sources are found attractive. Recognizing the nature of the scholarly enterprise, the student will then also find it easier to believe what is clearly the case, that what is *different* in artistic portrayal is not necessarily therefore *better*. The repainting of the past in colours which are *different* from those used by the authors of Kings, for example, will not necessarily be regarded as resulting in overall improvement. This will depend upon the perspective of the person who is making the judgment. For example, many scholars approach a book like Kings as if an important part of their task is to reinterpret what the authors of the book tell us about the past in terms of a closed system of thought where God does not act in the world, and where there can be no appeal to miracle as an explanatory account of events. Others offer reinterpretations which rely heavily on what people other than the authors of Kings, both ancient and modern, have to say about what was happening during the period in question. If the person making a qualitative judgment between portraits is, however, someone who happens in general to hold a view of the universe in which God does act in the world, and who happens in particular to regard the book of Kings as a particularly authoritative account of the past (as those who think it part of the Scriptures, for example, often so regard it), such modern reinterpretations are unlikely to be highly regarded. This person is unlikely to view the task of interpretation as involving the progressive expulsion of God from the book, and the progressive introduction of other, 'more objective' explanations for the course of Israelite history. Such a person is certainly not going to view the task as involving the reshaping of the book on the basis of material which was not at first included in it. The portrait as painted will rather be the object of study. The narrative will be taken seriously as a whole, in its relationship to the past.

This, however, is to stray into the subject matter of Chapter 6, which it would be unwise to do in advance of Chapters 4 and 5. Before we discuss faith again, we must first reflect on religion and religious teaching.

Further Reading

The best general introduction to biblical historiography is:

V.P. Long, *The Art of Biblical History* (FCI; Grand Rapids: Zondervan, 1994).

The following are also useful in different ways:

J. Goldingay, *Approaches to Old Testament Interpretation* (ICT; Leicester: Inter-Varsity Press, rev. edn, 1990), pp. 66-96. A good brief discussion of the Old Testament as historiography.

B. Halpern, *The First Historians: The Hebrew Bible and History* (San Francisco: Harper & Row, 1988). A more extended discussion.

K.L. Younger, Jr, *Ancient Conquest Accounts: A Study in Ancient Near Eastern and Biblical History Writing* (JSOTSup, 98; Sheffield: JSOT Press, 1990). Much of this excellent book is a difficult read, but there is a particularly good discussion of history and ideology in general on pp. 1-58, and a brief introduction to Assyrian ideology in particular on pp. 61-69.

Examples of recent books and articles on the history of Israel which have drawn a sharp distinction between narrative and history are:

G.W. Ahlström, 'The Role of Archaeological and Literary Remains in Reconstructing Israel's History', in D.V. Edelman (ed.), *The Fabric of History: Text, Artifact and Israel's Past* (JSOTSup, 127; Sheffield: JSOT Press, 1991), pp. 116-41.

G.W. Ahlström, *The History of Ancient Palestine from the Palaeolithic Period to Alexander's Conquest* (ed. D.V. Edelman; JSOTSup, 146; Sheffield: JSOT Press, 1993).

P.R. Davies, *In Search of 'Ancient Israel'* (JSOTSup, 148; Sheffield: JSOT Press, 1992).

N.P. Lemche, *Ancient Israel: A New History of Israelite Society* (The Biblical Seminar 5; Sheffield: JSOT Press, 1988).

K.A.D. Smelik, *Converting the Past: Studies in Ancient Israelite and Moabite Historiography* (OTS, 28; Leiden: Brill, 1992)

T.L. Thompson, *Early History of the Israelite People from the Written and Archaeological Sources* (SHANE, 4; Leiden: Brill, 1992).

For a more extended critique of this scholarship than is offered here, see:

I.W. Provan, 'Ideologies, Literary and Critical: Reflections on Recent Writing on the History of Israel', *JBL* 114 (1995), pp. 585-606, with the robust responses from Thompson and Davies which follow.

On the nature of historiography in general, see:

J. Clive, *Not By Fact Alone: Essays on the Writing and Reading of History* (London: Collins Harvill, 1990). A particularly illuminating and entertaining series of essays.

R.G. Collingwood, *The Idea of History* (Oxford: Oxford University Press, 1946).

R.H. Nash, *Christian Faith and Historical Understanding* (Grand Rapids: Zondervan, 1984), pp. 93-109.

P. Veyne, *Writing History: Essay on Epistemology* (trans. M. Moore-Rinvolucri; Manchester: Manchester University Press, 1984).

M. Stanford, *The Nature of Historical Knowledge* (Oxford: Basil Blackwell, 1986).

On analogy in particular:

W. Abraham, *Divine Revelation and the Limits of Historical Criticism* (Oxford: Oxford University Press, 1982), pp. 92-115.

On the nature of archaeology in particular, see:

F. Brandfon, 'The Limits of Evidence: Archaeology and Objectivity', *Maarav* 4.1 (1987), pp. 5-43.

D.V. Edelman, 'Doing History in Biblical Studies', in D.V. Edelman (ed.), *The Fabric of History: Text, Artifact and Israel's Past* (JSOTSup, 127; Sheffield: JSOT Press, 1991), pp. 13-25.

On Hezekiah and the Assyrian invasion of Judah:

K.A. Kitchen, *The Third Intermediate Period in Egypt (1100-650 BCE)* (Warminster: Aris and Phillips, 1973).

J.B. Pritchard (ed.), *Ancient Near Eastern Texts Relating to the Old Testament* (Princeton: Princeton University Press, 3rd edn, 1969), pp. 287-88. The text of the Rassam Prism Inscription of Sennacherib.

I.W. Provan, *Hezekiah and the Books of Kings: A Contribution to the Debate about the Composition of the Deuteronomistic History* (BZAW, 172; Berlin: De Gruyter, 1988), pp. 120-30, noting especially the extensive footnotes.

C.R. Seitz, *Zion's Final Destiny: The Development of the Book of Isaiah* (Minneapolis: Fortress Press, 1991), ch. 3.

4

THE BOOK OF KINGS
AND THE RELIGION OF ISRAEL

I noted in the last chapter that the telling of the history in
the book of Kings is dominated by the religious convictions of
the authors, and that the perspective from which they write
cannot be identified in a straightforward manner with that of
the Israelite community as a whole. The religion of Israel as
idealized in the book is not the same thing as the religion of
Israel as it was universally practised by Israelites. The distinction between the two has proved to be the starting point
for much hypothesizing about the nature of Israelite religion
in the pre-exilic period. In particular, it has become fashionable to claim that the 'Deuteronomists' (the authors of Kings)
have distorted reality with regard to Israelite religion in this
period. Their presentation of Israelite religion is said to be
tendentious and misleading.

The origins of this way of thinking about Kings lie in the
work of various nineteenth-century German scholars who
were interested in the history of Israel's religious development (e.g. de Wette, Reuss, Graf, Wellhausen). Out of this
context arose a general hypothesis about the history of
Israelite religion which understood it in its earlier period
(before and during the early monarchy) as knowing nothing
of any centralized, powerful priesthood, nor of any fully
fledged system of sacrifices, such as are described in books
like Exodus, Leviticus, Numbers and Chronicles. Early
Israelite religion was a much more informal, decentralized
affair. For scholars like Wellhausen, it was the 'natural'

period of Israel's religion, with spontaneity rather than structure as its hallmark. It was only towards the end of the monarchy that there was movement away from these early ideals, apparent in the demand for centralization of worship and sacrifices in Deuteronomy. Deuteronomy, on this view, is not what it presents itself to be—a book from the Mosaic age—but rather a seventh-century book associated with Josiah's reform as described in 2 Kings 22–23. It is the book of the law 'found' in the temple in Jerusalem, providing the basis for new departures in Israelite religion which were retrograde in that they severely restricted the spontaneity of earlier times. For Wellhausen, post-exilic Judaism represented the end-point of the process of decline that set in with Deuteronomy, natural and spontaneous worship having become impossible because of the accumulation of cultic and ritual laws. With this general view of Israel's religious development is associated a particular view of the development of the Pentateuch, which has come to be known as the Documentary Hypothesis. The earliest strata here, representing the early, natural period in religion, are the sources J and E (for example, many of the patriarchal stories in Genesis); next comes D (Deuteronomy); and finally there is P, the priestly source which introduces, among other things, much of the detailed cultic and ritual legislation.

The consequence of this general view of the history of Israelite religion for one's reading of the Deuteronomistic History is that the Deuteronomists' portrait of Israelite religion is not to be trusted. They have presented a picture which is at variance with reality in at least one centrally important respect (the importance of Deuteronomy before the seventh century). If this is the case, then we cannot necessarily depend upon their account in other respects. The history of Israelite religion must be reconstructed, rather than simply read off from the texts. In the modern climate which has been described in Chapter 3, where the biblical texts have become so thoroughly marginalized in the process of historical reconstruction, this has often meant in recent practice that a stance of radical doubt has been adopted towards the text. Many scholars apparently no longer believe that the Deuteronomists may be trusted at all as witnesses to Israel's

religious past, even in terms of what we might call basic distinctions between what is 'Yahwistic' religion and what is
not. In other words, what was once a fairly mild form of scepticism with regard to the biblical text has in recent times
become a marked scepticism. Where once it might have been
widely accepted, for example, that whatever else might be
true about Israelite religion, it was certainly true that basic
distinctions existed even in the earlier periods between
'Israelite' and 'Canaanite' religion, this is no longer the case.
It is increasingly the case, rather, that the Deuteronomists
are blamed for suppressing in their story a reality which was
far more complicated; a reality, for example, in which it was
quite acceptable for the worship of Israel's God to involve
images of various kinds. The Deuteronomistic vision of religion is increasingly presented, in fact, as a late retrospection
and an imposition on an earlier, very different reality. This is
connected with the increasingly popular late dating of many
Old Testament texts, particularly Deuteronomy, which would
now be regarded by some, not so much as the law-book of
Josiah's reform, but as the reform programme of the post-
exilic Jerusalem priesthood. Even many of those who still
identify Deuteronomy as Josiah's law-book would want to
argue that at least some of it comes from a time later than
Josiah's.

1. Examples from Kings

Lest we allow the focus of the discussion to slip away from
the book of Kings in particular, let us turn our attention to a
few examples of the kind of thing that is often said of this
book in discussions of Israelite religion.

1 Kgs 6.1-38 provides us with a detailed description of the
Solomonic temple, beginning with its external structure (6.1-
13) and moving on then to its internal arrangements (6.14-
35). Most attention is paid to the inner sanctuary (vv. 16,
19-32): its separation from the larger main hall (v. 16),
its measurements (v. 20), its decor (vv. 20, 29-30), its doors
(vv. 30-32), its altar (vv. 20, 22), and in particular its cherubim (vv. 23-28). In comparison, the other parts of the temple
receive only limited attention, although there is much

interest in the splendour of the decoration in general. The predominant word is 'gold' (vv. 20-22, 28, 30, 32, 35), but there is reference also to carvings of further cherubim (vv. 29, 32, 35) and, similarly, to carvings of gourds (vv. 18, a wild fruit; cf. 2 Kgs 4.39), open flowers (vv. 18, 29, 32, 35) and palm trees (vv. 29, 32, 35)—symbols, perhaps, of God's gift of fertility. Symbolism like this has played an important part in leading some scholars to the kind of conclusion that we have outlined above: that 'official' pre-exilic Israelite worship was not so different from the kind of worship that is condemned elsewhere in Kings as idolatrous (e.g. in such passages as 2 Kgs 17.7-20, with its emphasis also upon fertility rites). What is labelled and condemned in these places as Canaanite was in fact the indigenous, Israelite cult of Jerusalem.

1 Kgs 12.25-33 tells us of events in northern Israel immediately following the schism between Israel and Judah under Rehoboam. We are informed that the new Israelite king, Jeroboam, is afraid that the presence of the temple of the LORD in Jerusalem will undermine his kingship. He therefore resolved to build rival centres of worship within his own territory, in the far north (Dan) and in the far south (Bethel), infringing the prohibition in Deuteronomy 12; and he constructed two golden calves as focal points for worship at these sanctuaries. Moreover, he appointed illegitimate priests to service his Bethel sanctuary, blurring the important distinction between those set apart by God for priestly service (here Levites) and those simply of the people; and he created an illegitimate central festival like the festival held in Judah. The story evokes memories of Aaron; for he, too, having made his golden calf, built an altar and announced a festival on a date of his own choosing (cf. Exod. 32.5). And it was the Levites who on that occasion also were to be found distanced from the celebrations (Exod. 32.26). For the authors of Kings, Jeroboam is one of the worst of sinners, his sin a fateful event in the history of the northern kingdom (cf. 2 Kgs 17.21-23). It is often held, however, that Jeroboam has had a raw deal from these authors. It is argued that he did not in fact initiate idolatrous worship in Israel at all, but in effect only substituted the calves for the ark and the cherubim in a slightly different version of the worship of the LORD in

Jerusalem. He is not so much wicked, it is claimed, as misunderstood, even misrepresented; what he really wanted was for Israel to worship the LORD through the medium of the calves. The great distance that the authors of Kings have set between true worship of Yahweh and Jeroboam's worship is a distortion of reality.

Finally, various verses in Kings appear to refer or allude to a goddess figure, Asherah, and to cultic objects apparently associated with her (cf. 1 Kgs 14.15, 23; 15.13; 16.33; 18.19; 2 Kgs 13.6; 17.10, 16; 18.4; 21.3, 7; 23.4, 6, 7, 14, 15). The references are always negative, the authors of Kings clearly regarding worship involving Asherah/the asherim as incompatible with authentic worship of the LORD. For many scholars, however, this is to view the religion of monarchic Israel from the perspective of a much later period. Where the Deuteronomists criticize the religion of Rehoboam of Judah's time, for example, because it was conducted according to the abominations of all the peoples that the LORD dispossessed before the Israelites (1 Kgs 14.21-24), it is now maintained rather that it was '...in harmony with its time, no more and no less' (Ahlström 1993: 561). On this view, worship of Asherah is far from being an alien element in Israelite religion, the corruption of an original purity. Asherah was worshipped by the Israelites from the earliest times, and even had a place in the Jerusalem temple itself (e.g. Ahlström 1993: 477). Particularly on the basis of inscriptions found at Khirbet el-Qom and Kuntillet 'Ajrud, we may now say that Asherah was the female consort of the LORD in Israelite religion in much the same way that the goddess Athirat/Ashratu appears in special relationship to the chief deity of whichever other ancient Near Eastern culture she appears in. The radical dissociation of Asherah and the LORD which we now find in the book of Kings represents, on this view, a distorting and revisionist Deuteronomistic reading of the past.

2. Revisionism Revisited

In offering an assessment of this kind of treatment of the book of Kings, I begin, not with the interpretation of the passages just mentioned, but with a much wider issue. It is an obvious feature of the history of the modern sub-discipline known as 'history of Israelite religion' that scholars' assessments of what is 'true' or 'authentic' or even 'original' in the religion of Israel have been bound up with the broader philosophical and cultural currents in which they have found themselves afloat. It is evident in retrospect, for example, just how far Wellhausen's reconstruction and interpretation of the historical process was influenced by a Romanticism which regarded the early period of any people's history as the true expression of that people's spirit; by a general Protestant context in which spontaneity was valued over ritual; by a particular form of Lutheranism that led him to take a negative view of Law; and by a political culture that led him to view Israel's monarchic period particularly favourably, in contrast to its postexilic period. This does not necessarily mean that his individual insights about the Old Testament are flawed. It does demonstrate, however, just how far the scholarly task, in so far as it involves something as subjective as 'reconstruction', is far from being a purely objective enterprise. There is always a danger that what we 'reconstruct' will turn out to be simply the externalized figment of our own imagination. We shall find in 'the past' a reflection of and validation for what is important to us in the present.

It is worth remembering this especially when we turn to consider modern reconstructions of Israel's religious past. One might well ask if it is really only coincidence that it is in a time of religious pluralism, when distinctions between religions are underplayed and the notion that some religions might be more true or better than others is increasingly ruled out of court and considered politically incorrect, that we should be told that Israel's religion was not so different from that of its neighbours after all. One might well go on to ask whether it is also only coincidence that it is in a time of widespread heart-searching among readers of the Bible about the 'maleness' of God that it should (conveniently) turn out, after all, that Israelite religion had a female goddess. Of course, it could be that both these assertions are true. It could be that they have always been true, and that we have simply had insufficient information hitherto, or have been so culturally and religiously inhibited that we have not seen the truth. It is, nevertheless, worth pausing for thought. The wreckage of past scholarly ships should alert us to look for rocks.

a. *Was There a Book of Deuteronomy before the Time of Josiah?*

With these thoughts in mind we may return to consider the crucial question, from the point of view of our interest in Kings, whether the case has in fact been clearly made and should unquestioningly be accepted that Deuteronomy is indeed essentially a book that is no earlier in date than the seventh century. I say 'essentially' because it matters little for the present discussion whether the book of Deuteronomy in the precise form that we know it came into being at an earlier date, or rather grew from a smaller and earlier core into its present proportions. All we need to know is whether there was an early Deuteronomy which in its basic religious and legal perspectives was essentially the book that we now know.

I ask this question at a time when the general hypothesis advanced by Wellhausen in respect of the Pentateuch has come under serious scrutiny, with scholars like Rendtorff and Whybray offering radical criticism of it. It increasingly seems that it is only an *a priori* commitment to the Documentary Hypothesis as a whole in the midst of enormous disagreement about every aspect of the detail that continues to hold some scholars so steadfastly to it. Along with that commitment goes a commitment to the older literary-critical approach which Wellhausen employed in arriving at his conclusions. The more one believes this kind of approach to the biblical text to have been undermined by the newer literary approaches described in Chapter 2, the less one will see the need to move in Wellhausen's direction. Wellhausen himself affirmed, for example, that if the sources J and E could not be found in the Joseph story (Gen. 37–50) it would call in question his whole theory about the Pentateuch. If one doubts that J and E can be found there—and it is widely doubted (see, for example, C. Westermann, *Genesis 37-50* [London: SPCK, 1987], pp. 19-26), especially by those more convinced than their predecessors of the essential coherence of the narrative—then Wellhausen himself invites us to draw the awkward conclusion.

What, then, of Deuteronomy? How firm is the evidence that this is a book that first appears only towards the end of the era described by the book of Kings, rather than a book composed in earlier times? Here we must first remind ourselves that Kings itself regards Deuteronomy as predating the Solomonic era. I noted in Chapter 1.3.c how right at the beginning of Kings Solomon is charged by David with keeping the law of Moses (1 Kgs 2.3). From this point on, the impression is unsurprisingly created that this same law was generally available to the various kings of Israel and Judah, whether they paid attention to it or not. Jehu is criticized for not keeping it with all his heart (2 Kgs 10.31); Amaziah commended for acting in accordance with it (14.6); and the Israelites in general condemned for ignoring it (17.13; cf. also 17.34, 37). In 2 Kings 18 Hezekiah is commended for keeping the law of Moses (v. 6), after a description of religious reform which clearly recalls Deut. 12.1-7. It is nowhere implied that these kings conformed themselves to this law by chance, nor failed to do so through ignorance. Their success and failure in keeping the law had to do, rather, with will-power.

Nor does anything in the account of Josiah's reign as it stands contradict this earlier material in its point of view. We discover in 2 Kings 22–23 that the book of the law has been lost or concealed. There is no reason to think that this loss or concealment is being presented as anything other than a recent event, occurring during the long reign of the apostate Manasseh. If one were to hypothesize, it is certainly not difficult to imagine why it should have left the public domain during this period, given that it is a book whose laws Manasseh is portrayed as systematically infringing, and whose authority over kings he refuses to acknowledge (cf. Deut. 17.18-20). Nor is it difficult to understand that a child brought up in a royal court that has been apostate for fifty-seven years and that has subjected all opposition to a reign of terror should be unaware of this book's stipulations. Be that as it may, the book of Kings does not present Josiah as the first to *know* about Deuteronomy, but only as the first fully to do as it says. He is the ideal king of Deut. 17.20 who does not

'turn' (Heb. *swr*, as in 2 Kgs 22.2) from the law to the right or
to the left. This is only the first of many references in 2 Kings
22–23 that link Josiah with the law of Moses in general and
the figure of Moses in particular, presenting him as a king
who transcended even David and Hezekiah in his faithfulness to God (cf. 23.21-25).

What are the grounds for holding that this picture is fundamentally wrong? Is there evidence to the contrary, that no
Deuteronomic law-code existed in the period that Kings
describes? It is certainly true that many scholars offer literary-critical analyses of 2 Kings 22–23 which seek to dissolve
the connection between the law-book and Josiah's reform,
arguing that these have only secondarily been associated
with each other (e.g. Würthwein). Yet even scholars who do
not necessarily subscribe in general to newer narrative-criti-
cal approaches have found the older literary-critical kind of
analysis unconvincing in respect of 2 Kings 22–23.
Engagement with the newer approaches only decreases the
amount of faith one is able to place in the proposed 'reconstructions' of these chapters; and even if they were accurate,
what is secondary is not necessarily thereby untrue (see
Chapter 3). So why, we may repeat, is the portrait in Kings
with regard to the book of the law to be regarded sceptically?
Is it because there are other aspects of the text or evidence
from outside the text that are inconsistent with the general
picture painted here?

b. *Non-Deuteronomic Religion in the Monarchic Period*
Here I must return to consider the specific examples from
Kings that I first discussed above. Do we find reason from
this kind of material to conclude that the authors of Kings
are not trustworthy witnesses to Israel's religious past?

Our first example was that of the fertility symbolism of the
temple, which has led some to the view that 'official' pre-
exilic Israelite worship was not so different from the kind of
worship that is condemned elsewhere in Kings as idolatrous.
If this were clearly the case, then we would have to conclude
that the authors of Kings had indeed misled us. These
authors are happy to concede that 'official' pre-exilic Israelite
worship was *from time to time* in Judah not so very different

from idolatrous worship. They clearly present the early Solomon, however (1 Kgs 3.2-14 notwithstanding), as a faithful worshipper of Israel's God according to their own Deuteronomistic understanding of what this means. If he in fact built a temple that was not consistent with such an understanding, this would be a problem.

We are not driven to such a conclusion, however. That *popular* Israelite religion was indeed deeply influenced (the authors of Kings would say 'corrupted') by Canaanite fertility religion is beyond doubt. Nor can there be any doubt but that the authors of Kings did believe that the Solomonic temple contained certain cult items that later came to be seen as idolatrous. Thus the Mosaic bronze snake, Nehushtan, although not presented in Old Testament tradition as having originally been made for worship, appears nevertheless as the object of idolatrous worship in Hezekiah's day (cf. 2 Kgs 18.4). This only demonstrates, however, that the symbolism of the snake (a fertility symbol possibly associated elsewhere with the goddess Asherah) was open to misconstrual in Jerusalem in periods when the fertility cult was resurgent (the reigns of the later Solomon; Rehoboam and Abijam; Jehoram and Ahaziah; Ahaz). It does not demonstrate that the snake was understood in such a way from the beginning of temple worship. Nor does the symbolism of the temple in general require us to believe that it was from the start self-consciously syncretistic. The same symbol can signify differing things within differing systems of thought. We cannot assume, simply on the basis of analogy with other cultures *in general*, that we just 'know' what a symbol means in a *particular* culture at a *particular* time. Even where we may suspect a cross-cultural connection, the *context* in which the symbol is used can make all the difference. In other words, even if we wished to interpret some of the symbolism of the Solomonic temple in terms of 'Canaanite' religion (and 1 Kgs 6–7 itself gives us no explicit warrant for doing so), the real question is whether these symbols were not *from the start* recontextualized so that they embodied the claim that in fact it was the LORD, and not the god Baal, who was the giver of fertility (the point at issue in 1 Kgs 18); the LORD, and not the king, who was the establisher and maintainer of the cosmic order.

Our second example was that of Jeroboam: the worst of
sinners, or the victim of misrepresentation? The dogmatism
with which the latter position is sometimes asserted is such
that it is difficult to keep clearly in view the extent to which
its basis lies in speculation rather than in evidence. The
opposite position has been affirmed with equal force—that
Jeroboam deliberately set out to lead his people (back) into
Canaanite worship, and chose his symbols carefully with
that end in mind. The real curiosity of the claim about misrepresentation, however, lies in its suggestion that what
'actually happened' (Jeroboam encouraging worship of the
LORD via the calves, on this view) is not 'actually' idolatry at
all. From whose point of view? It is certainly idolatry so
far as passages like Deut. 4.15-24 are concerned. To worship
the LORD using representations of him is not to worship
him at all, but to worship 'other gods' (1 Kgs 14.9). Whatever
Jeroboam *thinks* he is doing with his calves, it is from this
point of view idolatry; and it is already clearly associated
with the worship of Canaanite deities in 1 Kgs 14.15. If what
is meant, on the other hand, is that this would not have been
viewed as idolatry by many of Jeroboam's contemporaries,
then no doubt this may be true. The authors of Kings do not
make explicit claims about what was happening in the minds
of Jeroboam's contemporaries. Even if it were so, however,
the claim that the distinction made in Kings between true
worship of Yahweh and Jeroboam's worship represents a 'distortion of reality' is a strange one, unless Jeroboam's (supposed) opinion about what he was doing is simply identified
with 'reality'.

Finally, what of Asherah? Here again it should be noted
just how limited are the data upon which the 'reconstruction'
is built. Archaeologists may or may not have discovered evidence outside the biblical texts that some Israelites regarded
Asherah as the LORD's consort. This is a highly controversial
area of debate. Those with expertise in such matters are
quite unable to agree on the interpretation of either of the
inscriptions mentioned above, and the Khirbet el-Qom
inscription in particular is exceedingly problematic (see
Wiggins 1993: 163-81). The point, however, is this: the dis-
covery that some Israelites in certain places and at certain

times regarded Asherah as the LORD's consort and/or worshipped her would not in itself be inconsistent with the portrait of Israelite religion that is painted in Kings. The authors
of Kings are quite ready to concede that for much of Israel's
history the religion of Israel was syncretistic. They would not
concede that it was syncretistic in origin and in essence, of
course; but then discoveries such as those described do not
prove that this was the case. There is, in fact, no hard evidence that establishes that the worship of Asherah was an
indigenous and original feature of Israelite religion (although
the biblical tradition does suggest that many Israelites were
in general syncretists from early times, for example, Exod.
32). There is likewise no evidence that demonstrates that
Asherah found a place in the Jerusalem temple before the
time of Manasseh—and even then, the evidence is only that
of the biblical text itself (2 Kgs 21.7), which forthrightly
condemns what is seen as an innovation. Such evidence as
we have (or may have) from outside our biblical texts indi-
cates only that some Israelites worshipped both Asherah and
the LORD—and this is precisely what the biblical texts themselves tell us.

3. Conclusion

The fact appears to be that the continued dating of Deuteronomy in the seventh century and/or later has more to do with
the reassertion of scholarly tradition than with compelling
argument. It has certainly not been demonstrated that the
data available to us are inconsistent with the biblical portrait
of a book of ancient origin which was nevertheless often dis-
regarded—even if the possibility must be considered that our
present book of Deuteronomy has indeed been expanded and
developed (like other biblical books) over a longer period of
time. Like the Documentary Hypothesis overall, then, the
older critical dating of Deuteronomy survives (where it does
so) more because of the force of continuing shared belief than
because of convincing detailed argument. There appears also
to be a similar shared perspective about the 'true' nature of
Israelite religion generally which is driving the interpretation of the evidence of both text and artifact when a book like

Kings is discussed. In fact, however, there is nothing in the
evidence, textual or artifactual, that clearly demonstrates
that the account of Israelite religion that appears in Kings is
'misleading'. The story found here is a story told from a particular point of view, certainly; but as we saw in Chapter 3,
this fact of itself does not make any description of the past
intrinsically flawed. The authors themselves fully acknowledge that people did not always or generally live up to the
ideals that the story expresses. One wonders, then, why it is
that these 'Deuteronomists' have gained such a bad press in
recent scholarly writing as distorters of reality.

With the general considerations of the opening paragraph
of section 2 above in mind, we may well ask how far this judgment has to do, not so much with demonstrable tension
between their picture of the past and 'what actually happened' in the past, but with the tension that clearly does exist
between the Deuteronomistic perspective on religion and the
perspective of many modern scholars who encounter it. The
latter often work within a cultural context that is fundamentally individualistic and relativistic in its approach to religion and life. Individuals decide what is true and right for
them, and no one else has any right to say that they are
wrong. The authors of Kings, on the other hand, are working
with ideas of what is true and right which they believe to
have considerably more objective reality, being revealed by
God through Moses. They are quite prepared to evaluate
their people's past in terms of this standard, and the question
of what individual Israelites (or indeed groups of Israelites)
might have thought about this is irrelevant. Given that, in
recent work on the religion of Israel, the evidence all too
often does not bear out the proffered interpretation of it, one
suspects that much of the vilification heaped upon the biblical authors therein finds its real source, not so much in any
demonstrable 'facts' about their distortion of the past, as
in a fundamental lack of sympathy with what they are say-
ing. In other words, the 'reality' in relation to which the
Deuteronomists are problematic is not so much historical
reality in respect of Israel, but rather present reality in
respect of much of the scholarly community. The remaking of
the past that is involved in the kind of 'reconstruction' that

has been described in this chapter is required, not so much because of Deuteronomistic distortion, but because there is a need for a past that is more acceptable in the present. There are important lessons here, it seems, for all those who would be students of the past in general and of Israel's past in particular.

Further Reading

On Israelite religion in the period covered by the book of Kings:

M. Barker, *The Older Testament: The Survival of Themes from the Ancient Royal Cult in Sectarian Judaism and Early Christianity* (London: SPCK, 1987). A book that develops the idea that Israel's pre-exilic religion was misrepresented as 'Canaanite' and suppressed by the Deuteronomists, the older ways surviving only in the themes and images of some later pseudepigraphic writing (notably the book of Enoch).

Y. Kaufmann, *The Religion of Israel: From its Beginnings to the Babylonian Exile* (trans. and abridged M. Greenberg; New York: Schocken Books, 1960). A book that takes the traditional view of Israelite religion, that there was a fundamental difference between worship of the LORD and worship of non-Israelite deities.

M.S. Smith, *The Early History of God: Yahweh and the Other Deities in Ancient Israel* (San Francisco: Harper & Row, 1990). A useful introduction to many of the issues discussed in this chapter, which develops the line that Israel's religion evolved from worship of the LORD as a primary deity among many to a fully defined monotheism where the LORD was sole God.

On Asherah in particular:

S.A. Wiggins, *A Reassessment of Asherah: A Study according to the Textual Sources of the First Two Millennia* BCE (AOAT, 235; Neukirchen–Vluyn: Neukirchener Verlag, 1993).

On the history of the history of Israelite religion:

F.W. Golka, 'German Old Testament Scholarship', in R.J. Coggins and J.L. Houlden (eds.), *Dictionary of Biblical Interpretation* (London: SCM Press, 1990), pp. 258-64.

On the weaknesses of the Documentary Hypothesis:

R. Rendtorff, *The Problem of the Process of Transmission in the Pentateuch* (JSOTSup, 89; Sheffield: JSOT Press, 1990). A much briefer treatment of the issues is found in his 'The "Yahwist" as Theologian? The Dilemma of Pentateuchal Criticism', *JSOT* 3 (1977), pp. 2-9.

R.N. Whybray, *The Making of the Pentateuch: A Methodological Study* (JSOTSup, 53; Sheffield: JSOT Press, 1987).

For an alternative account of the data most important to traditional accounts of the development of the Pentateuch:

R.W.L. Moberly, *The Old Testament of the Old Testament: Patriarchal Narratives and Mosaic Yahwism* (Minneapolis: Fortress Press, 1992).

On the date of Deuteronomy:

R.E. Clements, *Deuteronomy* (OTG; Sheffield: JSOT Press, 1989), pp. 69-83. A good introductory discussion which sees the origins of Deuteronomy as lying in ancient tradition while understanding the period of literary composition as beginning in the seventh century BCE.

5

THE BOOK OF KINGS
AS DIDACTIC LITERATURE

The book of Kings is a narrative about the past. It is not only
a narrative about the past, however, but also a narrative
which seeks to teach its readers a number of things about
God and God's ways. We turn next, therefore, to consider the
main outlines of the theology of the book of Kings. A brief
narrative summary is in order first of all.

The book of Kings opens with the struggle over which of
David's sons should succeed him to the throne. Solomon
emerges victorious over Adonijah, and is given instructions
by David about how he should rule (1 Kgs 1.1–2.11). He
should keep the Law of Moses, so that the LORD will keep his
promise to David of an everlasting dynasty over Israel; and
he should act as a man of wisdom. The succeeding narrative
is constructed around these two ideas of wisdom and law
(2.12–11.43). For much of the time Solomon's wisdom func-
tions in a positive way, as the people of Israel enjoy the prosperity and peace of the Solomonic empire and see the temple
of the LORD built in their midst. At both the beginning and
the end of his reign, however, it operates in a more self-inter-
ested way, as Solomon rids himself of those perceived to
threaten his hold on the throne and accumulates to himself
vast wealth. For much of the time, too, the king is presented
as someone committed to the LORD and his ways. Yet there
are from the beginning question marks about his complete
adherence to the law; and eventually he turns away and wor-
ships other gods. Surprisingly, however, his disobedience

does not lead to the end of the Davidic dynasty. A prophet announces that punishment will be deferred until the days of his son, who is to lose only part of the kingdom, rather than all of it. This alienation of part of Israel from David will itself not last forever. It is only a temporary phenomenon (1 Kgs 11, especially v. 39).

The dissolution of the empire is duly described, as Jeroboam son of Nebat leads northern Israel into independence from Rehoboam and Judah (1 Kgs 12.1-24). It is an exodus into slavery, however, as the northern kingdom is immediately captivated by other gods and never again succeeds in breaking free of their influence, whether they be the gods manufactured by Jeroboam (12.25-33) or those introduced from elsewhere (16.29-33). Prophets oppose the apostate kings, whose dynasties come and go, with greater or lesser speed, as the judgment of God falls upon them. The most notable of these prophets are Elijah and Elisha, whose activities take up a substantial part of the narrative throughout 1 Kings 17–2 Kings 13. They themselves in some respects mitigate the full force of God's wrath upon Israel, offering salvation in the midst of judgment. Final judgment is in any case slow in coming, because of God's promises and his compassion for his people (2 Kgs 10.30; 13.23). Eventually, however, it arrives; and northern Israel goes into exile in Assyria for her sins (2 Kgs 17).

Although the religious situation in Judah is initially no better than that in Israel (1 Kgs 14.22-24; 15.3-5), Judah's story is not thereafter one of continuous apostasy. Relatively good kings do rule in the gaps between the wicked kings (1 Kgs 15.9–22.50 [MT 22.51]; 2 Kgs 12.1 [MT 12.2]–15.38); and towards the end of the story, we meet two of the best kings there ever were (2 Kgs 18.1–20.21; 22.1–23.30)—kings who reform Israelite worship and obey and trust in God. Sin gradually accumulates, nevertheless; and although it at first appears that God will treat Judah with less severity than Israel because of his commitment to David, yet in the end this commitment only delays his judgment rather than averting it. The sins of Manasseh are too much to bear (2 Kgs 21); and Judah is duly exiled to Babylon (2 Kgs 24–25). The future of the Davidic line apparently hangs by the slender thread of a displaced ruler sitting at the table of the king of Babylon (25.27-30).

The theology of Kings can usefully be summed up under four headings.

1. The God of Israel

The first theme we must consider is the theme of God. We might describe the emphasis of the book of Kings in this way: that Israel's God is indeed God. The LORD is not to be confused with the various gods worshipped within Israel and outside—for these are simply human creations (1 Kgs 12.25-30; 2 Kgs 17.16; 19.14-19). They are part of the created order, like the people who worship them; and they are powerless, futile entities (1 Kgs 16.13, where the Heb. behind RSV's 'idols' literally means 'insubstantial things'; 18.22-40; 2 Kgs 17.15, where the case is the same as in 1 Kgs 16.13; 2 Kgs 18.33-35). The LORD, by contrast, is the incomparable Creator of heaven and earth (1 Kgs 8.23; 2 Kgs 19.15). He is utterly distinct from the world which he has created (1 Kgs 8.9, 14-21, 27-30, where he is neither truly 'in' the ark nor 'in' the temple; 18.26-38, where the antics of the Baal priests apparently imply belief in an intrinsic connection between their actions and divine action, while Elijah's behaviour implies quite the reverse), yet powerfully active within it. It is the LORD and no-one else, who controls nature (1 Kgs 17–19; 2 Kgs 1.2-17; 4.8-37; 5.1-18; 6.1-7, 27). It is the LORD, and neither god, nor king, nor prophet, who controls history (1 Kgs 11.14, 23; 14.1-18; 22.1-38; 2 Kgs 5.1-18; 10.32-33; 18.17–19.37). This latter point is perhaps illustrated most clearly in the way that prophets generally function within the book, describing the future before God brings it about (1 Kgs 11.29-39; 13.1-32; 16.1-4; 20.13-34; 2 Kgs 19.6-7, 20-34). Nothing can hinder the fulfilment of this prophetic word—although God himself, in his freedom, can override its fulfilment for purposes of his own (1 Kgs 21.17-29; 2 Kgs 3.15-27, where the ending to the story is somewhat unexpected). There is only one living God, then; and it is the LORD (1 Kgs 18.15; 2 Kgs 5.15).

2. True Worship

Secondly, as the only God there is, the LORD demands exclusive worship. He is not prepared to take his place alongside the gods, nor to be displaced by them. He is not about to be confused with any part of the created order. He alone will be worshipped, by Israelite and foreigner alike (1 Kgs 8.41-43, 60; 2 Kgs 5.15-18; 17.24-41). Much of Kings is therefore concerned to describe what is illegitimate worship. The main interest is in the *content* of this worship, which must not involve idols or images, nor reflect any aspect of the fertility and other cults of 'the nations' (1 Kgs 11.1-40; 12.25–13.34; 14.22-24; 16.29-33; 2 Kgs 16.1-4; 17.7-23; 21.1-9). There is subsidiary concern about the *place* of worship, which is ideally the Jerusalem temple, and not the local 'high places' (1 Kgs 3.2; 5.1–9.9; 15.14; 22.43 [MT 22.44]; 2 Kgs 18.4; 23.1-20). The book is also concerned to describe, however, the moral wrongs which inevitably accompany false worship. For as the worship of something *other than God* inevitably leads on to some kind of mistreatment of fellow mortals in the *eyes of God* (1 Kgs 21, where the kind of abandonment of God envisaged in Exod. 20 leads on to wholesale breach of the other commandments described there; 2 Kgs 16.1-4, noting v. 3; 21.1-16, noting vv. 6 and 16), so true worship of God is always bound up with obedience to the law of God more generally. By the same token, true wisdom is defined in terms of true worship and wholehearted obedience. It is not something which can be divorced from either (1 Kgs 1–11, where there is an extended play on the nature of true wisdom). Worship and ethics are two sides of the same coin, in Kings as elsewhere in the Old Testament.

3. A Moral Universe

Thirdly, as the giver of the law which defines true worship and right thinking and behaviour generally, the LORD is also one who executes judgment upon wrongdoers. The world of Kings is a moral world, in which wrongdoing is punished, whether the sinner be king (Solomon in 1 Kgs 11.9-13; Jeroboam in 14.1-18), or prophet (the unnamed Judaean in

1 Kgs 13.7-25; the disobedient man in 20.35-43), or an ordinary Israelite (Gehazi in 2 Kgs 5.19-27; the Israelite officer in 7.17-20). It is not a vending-machine world, however, in which every coin of sin which is inserted results in individually packaged retribution. There is no neat correlation between sin and judgment in Kings, for all that people are told that they must obey God if they are to be blessed by him (e.g. Solomon in 1 Kgs 2.1-4; Jeroboam in 11.38). This is largely because of the compassionate character of the Judge, who does not desire final judgment to fall upon his creatures (2 Kgs 13.23; 14.27), and is ever ready to find cause why such judgment should be delayed or mitigated (1 Kgs 21.25-28; 2 Kgs 22.15-20). God's grace is to be found everywhere in the book of Kings (1 Kgs 11.9-13; 15.1-5; 2 Kgs 8.19), confounding expectations which the reader might have formed on the basis of an over-simplified understanding of law. Sin can, nevertheless, accumulate to such an extent that judgment falls, not only upon individuals, but upon whole cultures, sweeping the relatively innocent away with the guilty (2 Kgs 17.1-23; 23.29–25.26).

4. The Divine Promise

This brings us finally to the theme of promise, which I must deal with at greater length. It is promise which is usually to be found at the heart of the LORD's gracious behaviour towards his people in the book of Kings. The two most important divine promises referred to are those given to the patriarchs and to David.

The patriarchal promise to Abraham, Isaac, and Jacob of descendants and everlasting possession of the land of Canaan clearly influences God's treatment of his people at various points in the story (2 Kgs 13.23, and implicitly in 1 Kgs 4.20-21, 24 [MT 4.20–5.1, 5.4]; 18.36), as well as lying in the background of Solomon's prayer in 1 Kgs 8.22-53, as that king looks forward to the possibility of forgiveness after judgment. The future-oriented aspect of the promise in this passage is interesting, because it is a promise which clearly lies in tension with the story's ending as we find it in 2 Kings 25, where disobedience has led to expulsion from the land and exile in a foreign empire. It seems that the true fulfilment of the promise still is thought to lie in the future, even though it has also played its part in the past.

The promise given to David that he should have an eternal dynasty shares in the same kind of tension, and indeed appears in the book in what may only be described as a curiously paradoxical form. For much of the narrative it provides us with an explanation as to why the Davidic dynasty survives, when other dynasties do not, *in spite of* the disobedience of David's successors (1 Kgs 11.36; 15.4; 2 Kgs 8.19). It is viewed, in other words, as unconditional. Judah's fate is not to be the same as Israel's, Jerusalem's fate is to be different from Samaria's, because God has promised David a 'lamp', a descendant who will always sit on his throne. Thus when Solomon sins the Davidic line does not lose the throne entirely, but retains 'one tribe' (11.36) in the meantime, with the prospect of restoring its dominion at some time in the future (11.39). When Abijam sins, likewise, his son still retains the Judean throne (15.4). The background here is evidently the promise to David as it is recorded in 2 Samuel 7, where the sins of David's descendants are to be punished by the 'rod of men' rather than by the kind of divine rejection experienced by Saul (2 Sam. 7.14-16). It is this promise that makes the ultimate difference between Davidic kings and those of other royal houses throughout much the book of Kings, and it makes the Judean dynasty unshakeable even while the dynasties of the northern kingdom are like 'reeds swaying in the water' (1 Kgs 14.15). The dynasty survives *in spite of* the disobedience of David's successors. At other times, however, the continuance of the dynasty is made *dependent upon* the obedience of David's successors (1 Kgs 2.4; 8.25; 9.4-5). The promise is treated as conditional. It seems that as the book progresses it is this latter view which prevails, as accumulating sin puts the promise in its unconditional aspect under too much stress, and in the end brings God's judgment down upon Judah just as severely as upon Israel (2 Kgs 16.1-4; 21.1-15; 23.31–25.26). And yet— Jehoiachin lives (2 Kgs 25.27-30). What is the significance of this fact?

Here we must reflect upon an important area of disagreement among interpreters of Kings, which has to do with the extent to which the book in the form that we have it looks optimistically to the future, and what the nature of any future hope might be. The two poles of the debate are perhaps represented by Noth (1981: 89-99), who argues that Kings is fundamentally a pessimistic work designed simply to tell the story of Israel's downfall and of the end of her monarchy; and von Rad (1962: 334-47), who finds an unresolved tension in the book between judgment and hope, the latter being a messianic hope based on the promise to the house of David of an everlasting dynasty. The closing verses of 2 Kings (25.27-30) represent a hint that the Davidic line will one day be restored through a descendant of Jehoiachin, who remains alive in Babylon. Of those many scholars who have disagreed with Noth in his reading of the book, few have felt able to go as far as von Rad. Even where interpreters have agreed that some hope is expressed (e.g. Wolff 1975: 83-100, who contends that in the Deuteronomistic History as a whole there is a pattern of repentance and forgiveness which suggests that the author still held out hope for a restoration of God's blessing), they have not generally highlighted messianism as an important strand of that hope (although there are exceptions, e.g. Childs 1979: 281-301). If hope exists at all in Kings, most believe it has been 'democratized'. Kingly figures belong to the unsatisfactory past from which Israel must now break free in corporate dependence upon the God who restores from exile.

Yet there is perhaps more to be said in support of von Rad than has often been thought. It is true that the closing verses of 2 Kings might of themselves be taken simply as the final nail in the coffin which the authors have so skilfully been preparing for Israel throughout the preceding chapters of the book. Solomon's glory has in the end departed to Babylon, on this view. The empire has dissolved. The Babylonian king has destroyed Solomon's city, his palace and his temple; he controls his empire, and he possesses all his wealth. Now Solomon's last-surviving successor (so far as we know) sits, amply provided for, at the Babylonian king's table—the great symbol of imperial power (cf. the high profile of Solomon's table in 1 Kgs 4.27 [MT 5.7]). He sits, he eats, and then (it is implied) he dies. The exiles (it is also implied) ought to

behave in the same way, accepting the advice of Gedaliah to
the people in Judah: 'Settle down...serve the king...and it
will go well with you' (2 Kgs 25.24). Such a reading of the end
of 2 Kings of itself is entirely possible. In the context of the
book of Kings taken as a whole, however, it is difficult to
believe that this is all there is to it; and that is the immediate
context, of course, in which 2 Kgs 25.27-30 must be read. We
cannot read the final words of the story without due attention to all the words which have preceded them and prepared
us for them.

The first thing to notice here is the simple fact that the
authors of Kings have chosen to tell us that Jehoiachin lived
on at all (in contrast to Jehoahaz, 2 Kgs 23.34), when they
could have allowed him to dwell in obscurity (with Zedekiah,
2 Kgs 24.18–25.7). They did not need to recount this part of
Jehoiachin's tale. They have also chosen to contrast the fate
of Jehoiachin's family (exile, 24.15) clearly with that of
Zedekiah's (death, 25.7). It is Zedekiah, and not Jehoiachin,
who ends up effectively as the 'eunuch in Babylon' that
Isaiah had foreseen (20.18), a mutilated man deprived of
heirs who might later claim the throne. Jehoiachin, by contrast, has living descendants. The significance of this mere
fact is more clearly seen when we consider the whole movement of the narrative in 2 Kings up to this point.

Throughout the initial stages of this second section of the
book, the reader still awaits the judgment which Elijah has
prophesied will fall upon Ahab's house (1 Kgs 21.17-29)—
judgment unexpectedly delayed, in the first instance, by
Ahab's own remorse when confronted by its announcement.
The delay is sufficiently long to allow the kingdom of Judah
to be drawn into Israel's sins. After two relatively righteous
kings (Asa, Jehoshaphat), we discover in 2 Kings 8.16-29
that Judah has found herself with two kings who share with
Ahab's children both their names (Jehoram, Ahaziah) and
their penchant for idolatry. The disease in Ahab's household
has proved infectious, carried south by his daughter (2 Kgs
8.18). Intermarriage has again wreaked its havoc (cf. 1 Kgs
11.1-8; 16.31-33). Yet God has promised David a 'lamp'
(2 Kgs 8.19). Here we find the reappearance of the motif
mentioned above which has already been seen twice in

1 Kings (11.36; 15.4)—the reappearance of the promise which makes the ultimate difference between Davidic kings and others.

It is certainly this promise which makes the difference in 2 Kings 9–11. When we are told about the Judean Ahaziah in 2 Kings 8.25-29, it seems at first that the promise is under threat. Although we anticipate that it will hold good for Jehoram's son as well as for his father, we note that it is not explicitly repeated in 8.25-29; and it is somewhat disconcerting to read in v. 26 that Ahaziah added only one year of life to the twenty-two which had passed by the time he succeeded to the throne. Did he die without an heir, we ask? What of the Davidic line after him? It is particularly disconcerting when we read alongside this information, in v. 25, that he came to the throne in Jehoram of Israel's twelfth year; for we know from 2 Kings 3.1 that Jehoram only ruled for twelve years. We are in the last moments of the house of Ahab; and it seems that the house of David, mixed up through marriage with this other, most wicked of royal houses, is to be caught up in the judgment. When we then read in 2 Kings 11.1 that after Ahaziah's death Athaliah the queen-mother 'proceeded to destroy the whole royal house', it seems that the end has indeed come. Yet this is not quite so. One royal prince remains to carry on the line (11.2); and against all the odds, he survives six years of his grandmother's 'foreign' rule to emerge once again as king in a land purified of the worship of foreign gods (11.3-20).

The significance of this for our reading of the end of the book of Kings becomes apparent once we remember how Hebrew narrative in general works (cf. the discussion of narrative patterning in Chapter 2) and how it is that the Ahab story in particular provides the framework within which 2 Kings 21–23 must be read. What is interesting here is that the characters of both Manasseh and Josiah are drawn in these chapters so as to remind us, each in his own way, of Ahab. Manasseh imitates Ahab by building altars to Baal (2 Kgs 21.3; cf. also the Asherah pole in 1 Kgs 16.33) and by worshipping idols (2 Kgs 21.11; cf. 1 Kgs 21.26). The judgment that will fall on Jerusalem because of Manasseh's sins is to be analogous to what happened to the house of Ahab

1 & 2 Kings

(2 Kgs 21.13). That was judgment, of course, which completely destroyed the royal house (1 Kgs 21.21-22; 2 Kgs
9–10; cf. 1 Kgs 14.10 and 21.21 for the only occurrences prior
to 2 Kgs 21.12 of 'I am going to bring...disaster'). It seems
from this that the Davidic line is to end after all, divine
promises notwithstanding. It seems that there will be no
escape, on this occasion, like the narrow escape of 2 Kings
11.1-3—that this time, identification with Ahab will lead the
house of David to Ahab's fate. What is said about the righteous Josiah does nothing to dispel this impression. Huldah's
words to him in 2 Kings 22.15-20 simply confirm what we
already know from the unnamed prophets of 2 Kings 21. It is
true that because Josiah has humbled himself before the
LORD (v. 19), he will not personally see all the disaster that is
to fall on Jerusalem. There is to be a delay of the kind that
we saw with Ahab, whose house was also spared for a while
because he tore his clothes and 'humbled himself' (1 Kgs
21.27-28). Manasseh's grandson, in other words, is now being
treated, as his grandfather was, like Ahab. Josiah's reaction
makes a difference—but only to him. The judgment which
has been announced will still surely fall, as it fell on the
house of the apostate predecessor.

These parallels drawn between the house of David and the
house of Ahab in 2 Kings 21–23 clearly imply that the
destruction of David's house will be total. There will be no
escape of the kind which occurred in Athaliah's day. The full
significance of the mere mention of Jehoiachin and his family
in the closing chapters of Kings now becomes apparent. He
reappears in the narrative in a manner strikingly reminiscent of the appearance of Joash after that earlier destruction
of the 'whole royal family'. He survives like Joash, unexpectedly, in the midst of carnage; and he represents, like Joash
during Athaliah's reign, the potential for the continuation of
the Davidic line at a later time, when foreign rule has been
removed. All is not yet necessarily lost, after all; the destruction of the family of the 'last king of Judah' (Zedekiah) does
not mean that there is no descendant of David left. As the
prayer of Solomon in 1 Kings 8.22-53 looks beyond the disaster of exile, grounding its hope for the restoration of Israel to
her land in God's gracious and unconditional election of

Abraham, Isaac and Jacob (cf. also 1 Kgs 17.36-37; 2 Kgs 13.23; 14.27); as it refuses to accept that God's words about the rejection of people, city and temple (e.g. 2 Kgs 21.14; 23.27) are his final words; so too 2 Kings 25.27-30 in its narrative context hints that the unconditional aspects of the Davidic promise may even still, after awful judgment has fallen, remain in force. They express the hope that God may indeed be found to be, in the end as in the beginning, a God of grace and not only of commandment; the hope that, God's wrath having been poured out upon good Josiah's sons, his (admittedly wicked) grandson might still produce a further 'lamp for Jerusalem'—as his (equally wicked) forefathers did (1 Kgs 11.36; 15.4; 2 Kgs 8.19). These closing verses of the book thus hang on tenaciously, in difficult circumstances, to the words of 2 Samuel 7.15-16: 'my love will never be taken away from him...your throne shall be established forever'.

Can such a hope reasonably be described as 'messianic?' It is certainly a hope focused on the unforeseen future—a time which is not this time. There is no sense in the book of Kings that the king of the future is anything other than a distant prospect. It is equally clear that the king who is sought is an ideal king. The book of Kings always measures its monarchs in terms of the ideal, finding almost all of them wanting in serious respects. If what is meant by messianic hope, then, is hope centred on an ideal Davidic king of the future, then the hope of the book of Kings certainly qualifies as such. It is entirely reasonable, in fact, to take the figures of the two least criticised Judaean kings, Hezekiah and Josiah, together with the early Solomon (criticized, but nevertheless blessed by God to an unparalleled extent), as indicating the shape of the ideal towards which the authors of Kings were looking— something which both Jewish and Christian interpreters of later times certainly appear to have done.

5. Is the Theology of Kings 'Deuteronomistic'?

On a number of occasions in this guide we have noted with interest the connections between the book of Kings and the book of Deuteronomy, and we have referred to Martin Noth's hypothesis about a Deuteronomistic (sometimes called a

Deuteronomic) History. It will come as no surprise to the reader, therefore, that the theology of Kings is often referred to as 'Deuteronomistic' (or 'Deuteronomic'). For the sake of brevity, I myself have sometimes referred to the authors of the book of Kings as Deuteronomists and their outlook as Deuteronomistic. The question now arises, however, as to whether this is a particularly helpful way of thinking about the book.

It is important to remember, first of all, that the hypothesis about the so-called 'Deuteronomistic History' remains precisely that—a hypothesis. It is all too easy to forget this, in view of the general scholarly tendency to refer to the 'Deuteronomistic History' as if it were currently sitting in a library somewhere and could be compared with the biblical texts that we actually possess. This tendency notwithstanding, it remains the case that we are dealing here with an intellectual construct, an imagined original work which pre-exists our extant biblical books and is certainly not coterminous with them.

It is equally the case that 'Deuteronomistic theology' is itself a scholarly abstraction. We nowhere find any such thing as 'Deuteronomistic theology' set out and expounded for our enlightenment in any ancient document. It represents the construct of scholars theorizing about the corporate views of the original authors of Deuteronomy–Kings (the Deuteronomistic 'circle' or 'school'), rather than the theology of any particular book in the 'Deuteronomistic History' taken as a whole in its present form—even the book of Deuteronomy itself (as the careful reading of Weinfeld, 1972, more than adequately illustrates). Particular books as we have them tend to display a much greater theological subtlety and complexity than we would expect to find if we approached them with a 'standard' view of Deuteronomistic theology clearly in mind. They also appear quite different from each other in their particular theological emphases (cf., e.g., Judges with Kings). The construction of a 'Deuteronomistic theology' characteristically involves the blurring of all such subtleties, complexities and differences in the course of extracting an 'essence' which is said to lie beneath them and which speaks of a relatively uniform ideological perspective on the world.

This perspective is then brought back to the texts as the key to understanding what they are about, material which differs in perspective from that of 'the Deuteronomists' being explained either as pre- or post-Deuteronomistic (e.g. in Noth's analysis of the History), or perhaps as the later contribution of members of the Deuteronomistic 'circle' who added their contributions from a slightly different (but still Deuteronomistic) point of view (e.g. in redactional theories of the Cross and Smend varieties).

The question that arises from this procedure is whether the phrase 'Deuteronomistic circle' might not better be reserved for the argument implied in the procedure itself than applied to the hypothetical originators of the biblical texts—for circular the argument certainly is. Why should we imagine that a group of 'Deuteronomists' existed at all? The answer, seemingly, is that the biblical texts imply as much, since they have been shaped by a relatively uniform ideological perspective on the world which has some connection with Deuteronomy. But is there not evidence in the texts, in fact, that the ideological perspectives therein are not entirely uniform, and sometimes far from being so? Then, the reply comes, the textual evidence is not to be taken very seriously, or at most it is to be understood as implying that the Deuteronomists had broad interests and worked over a long period of time. It is worth reflecting on just how seriously one ought to take such a selective approach to what the texts 'imply'. It is also worth asking just how broad 'Deuteronomistic interests' can be before the concept 'Deuteronomists' begins to lose any coherent sense. It is certainly important to note the extreme difficulty that scholars have had when they have tried to put any flesh on these skeletal and shadowy figures who are said to lie behind books like Kings and to be so crucial to their understanding. Some say they are Levites or priests, some say prophets, and some say the wise men of the Jerusalem court. When, in response to much of the work done in this area, we find many now characterizing the 'Deuteronomistic School' as a comprehensive movement to which people of varying traditions belonged, perhaps the time has come to ask whether the Deuteronomistic Hypothesis is being kept alive (like the

Documentary Hypothesis) more by the faith of the scholarly
community than by the quality of the arguments. Is the
Hypothesis the presupposition of scholarly inquiry or gen-
uinely its result? It is indeed difficult to know what to make
of a 'school' which seems, after all, to have no unified ideological perspective and no plausible social location. Is it *neces-
sary* to posit 'Deuteronomists' with a 'Deuteronomistic
theology' at all when thinking about the Former Prophets?
Why not think simply of a number of texts which in different
ways over the course of time have been written and edited by
those influenced, among other things, by the book of Deuteronomy, which happened to be an important part of Israel's
Scripture (cf. Schüssler-Fiorenza, 1985: 85-113, for an interesting discussion of the so-called 'Johannine School' which
raises issues similar to those discussed here, and which does
readers the service [p. 90] of recalling the somewhat acid
comment of B.H. Streeter: 'The word "school" is one of those
vague, seductive expressions which it is so easy to accept as a
substitute for clear thinking')?

This may seem a fine distinction. However, the evidence
which can be gathered from scholarly writing on books like
Kings since 'Deuteronomists' first arrived on the intellectual
horizon suggests otherwise. It suggests that it matters
greatly in terms of one's appreciation of the theology of such
books whether one approaches them with the construct
'Deuteronomistic theology' in mind, or whether one is prepared to study them for what they are, both in themselves
and in the totality of their connections with other biblical
texts (and not simply those with which they are imagined
once to have had intimate connections). Much can be missed
of the subtleties and complexities mentioned above, and
indeed of the inter-textual connections of such books, if they
are encountered by readers who already think have in mind
an overly precise picture of what they will find there. There
is in scholarly writing, for example, nowhere near the
emphasis on the importance of the book of Exodus for our
reading of the book of Kings that we find in the case of book
of Deuteronomy. Yet it is plainly the case, in spite of the fact
that they tend not to be emphasized by those bedazzled by
the 'Deuteronomists', that the connections between Exodus

and Kings are many and important (for the evidence, see in the first instance the Scripture index to my commentary on Kings, noted in the further reading for Chapter 1). The text requires to be read for what it is; and when it is so read, its true nature becomes apparent. The enduring hold which the Deuteronomistic theory retains on scholarship is, however, well demonstrated in the fact that even among scholars who are now more interested in reading the Old Testament books in their final form (which is presumably, on any theory of composition, a *post-Deuteronomistic* form) than in speculating about the history of their composition, terms like 'Deuteronomistic theology' and 'Deuteronomistic History' should still be so widely used. It seems that the construct, once embedded in the mind, is difficult to dislodge. Indeed, final-form reading can itself be led astray if the reader is too profoundly convinced that a unified 'Deuteronomistic ideology' is historical fact as well as scholarly hypothesis. Thus Nelson (1988: 39-48), who fully recognizes that the book of Kings contains material which undermines such ideology rather than sustaining it, is not thereby led to question whether it actually exists at all. Rather, he simply sets the 'rogue' material in contrast to what he describes as the 'straight deuteronomistic ideology' or the 'deuteronomistic party line' of other parts of the book. The question that really must be asked, of course, is where such 'straight deuteronomistic ideology' is actually to be found anywhere in the Old Testament. The answer appears to be 'nowhere'.

Perceptive readers will have noticed that I have not, in fact, quite answered the question which heads this section of the chapter. Rather in the manner of the thoughtful student during an exam, I have instead chosen to spend time unravelling the difficulties which the question itself raises. This is because the question, although comprehensible to many scholars, is no longer comprehensible to me. To answer it, I should need to know what was meant by 'Deuteronomistic'—and it is the very coherence of this idea that needs to be established.

Further Reading

For a readable introduction to the themes of the book of Kings:
T.R. Hobbs, *1, 2 Kings* (WBT; Dallas: Word Books, 1989).

On the (Deuteronomistic) theology of Kings:
B.S. Childs, *Introduction to the Old Testament as Scripture* (London: SCM
    Press, 1979), pp. 281-301.
M. Noth, *The Deuteronomistic History* (JSOTSup, 15; Sheffield: JSOT Press,
    1981), pp. 89-99.
G. von Rad, *Old Testament Theology* (1 vol.; Edinburgh: Oliver and Boyd,
    1962), pp. 334-47.
M. Weinfeld, *Deuteronomy and the Deuteronomic School* (Oxford: Oxford
    University Press, 1972).
H.W. Wolff, 'The Kerygma of the Deuteronomic Historical Work', in W.
    Brueggemann and H.W. Wolff (eds), *The Vitality of Old Testament
    Traditions* (Atlanta: John Knox, 1975), pp. 83-100.

On the way in which particular books of the 'Deuteronomistic History' dis-
    play their own theological subtlety and complexity:
J.G. McConville, 'Narrative and Meaning in the Books of Kings', *Bib* 70
    (1989), pp. 31-49.
J.G. McConville, *Grace in the End: A Study in Deuteronomic Theology*
    (Grand Rapids: Zondervan, 1993).
R.D. Nelson, 'The Anatomy of the Books of Kings', *JSOT* 40 (1988), pp. 39-
    48.

On the identity of the Deuteronomists:
R.E. Clements, *Deuteronomy* (OTG; Sheffield: JSOT Press, 1989), pp. 69-83.
G.H. Jones, *1 and 2 Kings* (NCB; 2 vols.; Grand Rapids: Eerdmans, 1984), I,
    pp. 28-44.

On constructing 'schools' out of texts, or reading them in:
E. Schüssler-Fiorenza, *The Book of Revelation: Justice and Judgment*
    (Philadelphia: Fortress Press, 1985), pp. 85-113. A discussion of the so-
    called 'Johannine School'.

On the messianic question:
I.W. Provan, 'The Messiah in the Book of Kings', in P.E. Satterthwaite *et al.*
    (eds), *The Lord's Anointed: Interpretation of Old Testament Messianic
    Texts* (Carlisle: Paternoster Press), pp. 67-85.

6

THE BOOKS OF KINGS
AND THE BIBLE

It is perhaps the most obvious feature of the book of Kings to
the modern reader that it forms part of the Scriptures of both
Judaism and Christianity. It might seem surprising, therefore, that consideration of 'The Book of Kings and the Bible'
should be left until the end of this guide, as if the biblical
contexts in which Kings is found are only of secondary importance in our understanding of the book. That is indeed the
position that modern Old Testament scholars have generally
adopted. The roots of this position lie in the eighteenth century, towards the beginning of modern critical work on Old
Testament texts. In his *Treatise on the Free Investigation of
the Canon* (1771–1776), for example, we find Johannes
Semler arguing that the theological approach to the Hebrew
canon which regards it as a unified body of authoritative
writings should be replaced by a strictly historical approach
which would establish its 'true' historical development. Since
the eighteenth century this idea has gained widespread
acceptance. The biblical texts tend often to be interpreted in
the first instance as more or less chance remnants of a previous stage of human history whose meaning is wholly determined by their individual and historical circumstances of
origin. The canon, on the other hand, is regarded as an arbitrary and late imposition on originally unrelated texts of
diverse originating circumstances. It is the construct of religious authorities, alien to and distorting of the essence of the
Old Testament. Consequently, the 'correct' way in which to

treat a book like Kings in the first instance is in isolation
from its current literary and theological context as part of
Scripture. At best, it may be allowable to treat it in the context of some such reconstructed entity as 'the Deuteronomistic History'. For many Old Testament scholars, however,
the task of interpreting a book like Kings in the context of
the Old Testament as a whole, or indeed of the Christian
Bible as a whole, is not properly part of the academic task. It
is, rather, part of the task of the minister or the theologian
who, by implication, is moving in the realm of faith rather
than of intellect (to accept this question-begging polarity for
the moment). This is why so many modern commentaries on
individual Old Testament books, for example, self-consciously avoid commenting on the way in which the wider
biblical contexts of the book affect our reading of it.

My own view, on the other hand, is much closer to that of
Brevard Childs (e.g. 1979, 1993), who has been so influential
in Old Testament scholarship in the recent past in rehabili-
tating the idea of canon. To maintain that canon represents
an arbitrary and late imposition on the Old Testament texts
which has no hermeneutical significance, Childs argues, is to
misrepresent reality. Canon is rather a complex historical
process within ancient Israel which entailed the collecting,
selecting and ordering of texts to serve a normative function
as Scripture within the continuing religious community. The
notion of canon, in other words, is intrinsically bound up
with the Old Testament texts as we have them, and should
be taken seriously by those who study them. We cannot in
fact do justice to a book like Kings, whether as academics or
as theologians (or as both), unless we recognize that this
book was intended by its authors to be read as Scripture
along with other Scriptures. To ignore the scriptural context
in which the book now sits is to ignore something which is
fundamentally important about its nature.

Childs' views are a matter of controversy among Old
Testament scholars, and have excited much impassioned
debate. It is important in the first instance, therefore, to
explore this matter of Scripture and canon further, by means
of a brief interaction with James Barr (1983), who in oppos-
ing Childs' canonical approach also helpfully restates what

we might call the modern critical view. This will enable us to form a judgment as to the relative merits of each case.

1. The Book of Kings and the Canon of Scripture

a. *Scripture and Canon*

Barr's general view is that biblical faith was not, in its own nature, a scriptural religion. Old Testament man related to God much more through holy persons and institutions and through a sort of direct personal and verbal communication with God, and little or not at all through pre-existing written and authoritative holy books. It was the Deuteronomic movement around the eighth and seventh century, in fact, that first began to make something like a 'Scripture' central to the life of Israel. It is at this point that we first find what we might describe as 'Scripture consciousness'. It is probably only in later times, however, that we begin to find within the Old Testament itself explicit references to a pre-existing Scripture as a source requiring to be explained and interpreted. It is certainly only in the last centuries before the coming of Christianity that we find a clearly defined holy written Law (Torah) and other books of profoundly authoritative religious status—much of the rest of what is now commonly referred to as the Old Testament. This change meant a fateful and all-important change in the character of Israelite religion which has had the consequent effect of leading Christians to misconceive Christianity also as a scriptural religion. The idea of Scripture is thus a relatively late phenomenon in Israel, and the idea of canon (in the sense of a precise definition of the Scriptures) later still. Torah was never in fact canonized in the sense that the New Testament was canonized. It simply arrived at supreme and authoritative status in the time of Ezra. Moreoever, while the religious authority of the prophetic writings pre-dates the recognition of the supremacy of Torah, the prophetic section of the canon was probably not closed early on. 'The Prophets' was initially a catch-all category for any non-Torah book that was holy Scripture, and it was still a fluid category even in the first century CE.

Is the general position which Barr is trying to defend here

in fact defensible? How can its central claims be substanti-
ated? It is asserted on several occasions in the course of the
argument that these claims are grounded in the Scriptures
themselves: that this reading of the past is true to the Bible
in a way that others are not. Yet the general contours of the
picture which Barr paints here are reminiscent of nothing so
much as that nineteenth-century theory about the history of
Israelite religion that I have already found reason to criticize
in Chapter 4. We may note in the course of the argument just
the same emphasis upon an early 'authentic' period of faith
(particularly symbolized by the prophets), a period which
then gave way to a later regressive period of book-dominated
religion, which in turn gave way to a renaissance in early
Christianity (albeit a renaissance cut short by Christian misunderstanding). Further reflection on Barr's claims does
nothing to dispel one's sense of doubt about this reconstruction. Why should we believe, for example—since Barr himself
acknowledges that many of the national–religious traditions
of Israel which later became Scripture were already central
and authoritative early on, and that Deuteronomy in particular already evidences Scripture consciousness—that
Scripture consciousness only began to be an important feature of the life of Israel around the eighth and seventh centuries BCE? The assertion depends partly on prior acceptance
of the questionable hypothesis also mentioned in Chapter 4
about the significance of the 'finding' of the book of the law in
2 Kings 22. It depends partly on an ungrounded assertion
about Israel's authoritative traditions not yet being separa-
ble in the early period from the general life of all the traditions of the community. What is lacking, however, is the hard
evidence that necessitates the view that texts later regarded
as having special status as Scripture were once *not* so
regarded, and were not already demarcated in respect of
other texts which did not have this status. It seems intrinsic
in the careful preservation and passing on of prophetic traditions, for example, that these traditions were already
regarded at the point of origin as especially significant.

  An important question here, as Barr himself rightly points
out, is whether there is the kind of cross-referencing between
our Old Testament texts, at some fundamental level within

these texts, which would suggest that they were actually formed in the midst of Scripture consciousness. He himself acknowledges that a great deal of cross-referencing is indeed to be found in the Old Testament. Again, however, his overall theory drives the interpretation of the evidence in a noticeable way. He insists that it is only *explicit* references to other Old Testament books as Scripture which count as evidence. He dismisses what he calls mere glosses, literary similarities and allusions, or cross-references which suggest only a rather loose relation between books and traditions. Why explicit references should be privileged in this way is unclear, particularly when it is evident that even in the later biblical period, when Barr acknowledges that Scriptures do obviously exist, such references are still nonetheless thin on the ground. Why other sorts of cross-reference should at the same time be downplayed to such an extent is also unclear. I noted in Chapter 2 the way in which cross-referencing was far from being a trivial or marginal feature of the book of Kings. It is quite evident that the story in Kings is told in precisely such a way that it gets the reader thinking about its broader scriptural context. The book of Kings is not unique in this respect. It is an intrinsic feature of the nature of our Old Testament narrative texts that they have come into their present form in relationship with each other and with Torah and prophetic texts. The very form in which they are written time and time again invites reference to these other Scriptures. It seems that we do possess, then, the kind of evidence of Scripture consciousness for which Barr is looking.

If the evidence for a marked discontinuity between the earlier period of biblical faith and the later is weak, so too is the evidence for the further marked discontinuity which Barr suggests between *Scripture*-consciousness and *canon*-consciousness. The point here is that even if he is right in his central claim that we cannot talk about a canonization process for the Hebrew Bible similar to that undergone by the New Testament—and this is largely an argument from silence—does this mean that no *canon-consciousness* existed? Is it, in fact, not implicit in the notion that a certain text is Scripture, that another text is not Scripture? Is this implicit notion not seen precisely in the position attained, however it was attained, by Torah and Prophets? The question here is not whether everyone agreed precisely which texts were Scripture and which were not. The question is whether the idea of Scripture itself implies the idea of limitation, of canon, even if the limits are not yet conceived as having been reached. Even Barr is not entirely clear on the point (1983: 57), affirming that a clear distinction between Scripture and non-Scripture 'very probably' did not exist even at the turn of the era, while maintaining that a description such as 'wide religious literature without definite bounds' is 'perhaps too vague' to capture the reality. Why he objects to the latter if he really believes the former is not at all clear. Does he believe that there were limitations set to the number of the Scriptures even before the line between Scripture and non-Scripture had been finally drawn? But does that not, then, imply that the notion of limitation is built in to the notion of Scripture? And what are we to make of his later concession (1983: 83) that there was '...back into early Old Testament times, a sort of core of central and agreed tradition, a body of writings already recognized and revered, which...functioned...in the same general way in which the canon of Scripture functioned for later generations...', and his acceptance that '...the whole nature of Israelite religion was canonical, that it depended on the selection of a limited set of traditions which were accepted and were to be authoritative in the community...'? It is not easy to find consistency here.

The idea of Scripture does itself imply the idea of limitation, of canon. The question of when and how the Old Testament canon was formally closed is another matter, which is not immediately relevant to the question of canonical consciousness. This is precisely the point Childs himself makes when discussing his use of the word 'canon'. He rightly insists that it makes sense to speak of an 'open canon', precisely because closure is only one element in the process of canon, and not constituitive of it. Scripture and canon cannot be sharply distinguished.

b. *Scripture and Faith*
We are drawn to the conclusion, then, that there is really no reason to adopt the view that texts later regarded as having

special status as Scripture were once *not* so regarded, and were not already demarcated in respect of other texts which did not have this status; and there is good reason to adopt a different view, which sees our Old Testament texts as gradually developing into their present form in concert with each other, as Scripture interpreted Scripture. We are drawn to the opinion, then, that Childs is right when he claims that canon does not represent an arbitrary and late imposition on the Old Testament texts, but is rather intrinsically bound up with the Old Testament texts as we have them. Canon consciousness does lie deep within the Old Testament literature itself. Canon cannot be shown to be an extraneous distortion of a more fundamental textual essence which can be recovered only by historical methods.

This conclusion is important not least because it allows the vast majority of readers of the book of Kings—those who read it as Scripture—to do so without being haunted by a sense of guilt that in doing so they are perhaps mistreating it in some fundamentally important way. Such a sense of guilt is part of the common experience of many students beginning academic Old Testament study, as they try to maintain the general perspective on the Bible which they brought with them to college or university, while at the same time wishing to be intellectually honest. It is not easy when it is continually stated or implied that its nature as Scripture is the least important feature of a book like Kings to continue to affirm that the reality is in fact fundamental. Even where students are encouraged simply to bracket out their religious convictions about the nature of the text for a while, perhaps with the promise that they may re-engage them after they have completed their academic (often implicitly meaning 'objective') study of the text simply as text, the problems are severe. For this 'academic study of the text as text' has all too often in the past involved the stripping away of precisely those 'secondary' features which make the text what it is as Scripture in its canonical shape. The text is transported by historical-critical study into the hypothetical past by destroying essential aspects of the vehicle which has, as it were, enabled its journey into the present. It is little wonder, as Childs has noted, that having damaged the vehicle in this way, historical critics have so often found themselves unable then to devise a way of relocating the text satisfactorily in any modern religious context at all. The text remains simply a text like any other, embedded firmly in the supposed historical context which gives it its meaning; and what was promised only as a temporary student dwelling place in no man's land becomes all too quickly and irrevocably a permanent, entrenched hall of residence.

The solution to the problem lies precisely in understanding that the position adopted in so much of modern Old Testament scholarship—that the 'true' or 'essential' nature of the biblical texts is to be found elsewhere than in their nature as part of Jewish or Christian Scripture—is by no means self-evidently true. We are, in fact, dealing here with something which is in large measure a presupposition about the nature of the biblical texts, rather than something which can be demonstrated. There is, of course, nothing wrong with presuppositions as such; everyone possesses them. What we see is always bound up with the context in which the seeing is done. The point to grasp, however, is that when students are asked to abandon, even temporarily, a religious perspective on the biblical text, they are not being invited onto neutral, objective ground, but into a different interpretative paradigm—a world where readers possess just as many presuppositions about the text as they do, but of a quite different nature.

There is nothing obviously superior about this paradigm, intellectually speaking. It is indeed possible to argue, as we have seen, that it does less than justice to important features of the texts as we find them. It is an exceedingly curious proposition, in fact, when one reflects upon it in the light of these texts as we find them, that the 'correct' academic way in which to treat a book like Kings is in isolation from its current literary and theological context as part of Scripture. The texts themselves certainly do not invite us to read them in this way. Once the curiosity is observed, the focus of academic endeavour may well begin to shift even if the reader concerned comes to the texts with no particular religious interest in them. Interpretation of a book like Kings in the context of the whole Bible may become at least as important as speculation about the history of its composition. Understanding how Kings contributes to the theology of the whole Bible may become at least as important as understanding how Kings might or might not express the theology of those hypothetical Deuteronomists. The emphasis will fall more on the relation of the parts to the whole, rather than on the parts construed as self-contained entities (or even on the sub-parts and sub-sub-parts construed as such, as has too often been the case in modern scholarship). The Book will be seen clearly as the context in which the individual books are to be read.

2. The Book of Kings and the Christian Bible

I have referred above to 'the whole Bible'; and I have intended through my choice of phrase to indicate in the first instance those Scriptures which are known to Christians as the Old Testament and to Jews as Tanak. The 'whole Bible' so far as Christians in particular are concerned, however, contains at the very least (leaving aside in particular the vexed question of the Apocrypha) a further important section called the New Testament. The literary and scriptural context in which Kings is read is, for Christian readers, now a larger one. In the context of the Christian Bible, the story of Kings is now part of the story which reaches all the way from Genesis to Revelation. We proceed, therefore, to consider a question specific to Christian readers only: what difference does it make having this Christian 'Book' as the context in which the book of Kings is set?

a. *The Old Testament and Christian Thought*
Some brief comments on the relationship of the Old Testament to Christian thinking are perhaps in order first of all. Historically the Old Testament was the Scripture of both Jesus and the early church, before there was any New Testament to speak of. The patristic church confirmed its status as Christian Scripture in the post-apostolic period, retaining its integrity by leaving the shape of the books in the Jewish canon largely unchanged and juxtaposing it with the New Testament writings rather than simply collapsing

the Bible into one. The Christian Bible has remained a Bible
of two testaments since then, even under the most severe of
cultural and religious pressures. Theologically, the fundamental connections between the testaments are clear, the
Old Testament telling of the God of Israel and his dealings
with his people and with the world—the God who in the New
Testament is identified as the father of Jesus Christ, the
head of his body which is a new people of God comprising
both Jew and Gentile. The God of both testaments is the
same God, and the people of God in each testament are analogous to each other, as any number of New Testament texts
bear witness. The Old Testament thus provides the essential
hermeneutical context for the writings of the New
Testament, and there is no evidence that these writings were
ever intended to be read apart from this context. The Old
Testament in this sense is founda-tional Christian Scripture,
not simply historically, but also theologically.

Just how important this foundation is can be seen in the
literary connections between the testaments. If it is true
within the Old Testament that the story is told in such a way
that events and characters in the later chapters recall events
and characters in the earlier chapters, by way of comparison
or contrast, then it is equally true that the way in which the
New Testament story is told has much to do with the Old
Testament. The level of intertextuality between the testaments is, in fact, much higher than has often been supposed,
as scholars are increasingly discovering. We may take as an
example here the stories of Simon and the Ethiopian in Acts
8.9-40, which Brodie (1986) has argued are modelled largely
on the Old Testament story of Naaman and Gehazi in
2 Kings 5. Luke, he maintains, has distilled the essence of
the Old Testament text and has used that essence as a skeletal framework around which he has grafted other material.
Naaman's status as 'great' and his misguided preference for
actions and objects that are great have been used in characterizing the negative figure of Simon; his status as foreign
royal official has been used to depict the Ethiopian. Naaman
arrives in Israel with royal backing, money, and a scroll, but
initially fails to do the one thing needed—establish appropriate communication with God's prophet. The Ethiopian

arrives in a similar way, and indeed, like Naaman, in a chariot. In both texts the foreign official washes and is renewed. In both texts the question arises as to whether the gift of God can be exchanged for money. Elisha refuses Naaman's attempt to pay him, but Gehazi is happy to cash in on the miracle. Simon thinks that he can buy spiritual power. Both are confronted about their attempt to commercialize the gift; both are described in their wrongdoing as being (or fated to be) in the grip of a powerful negative force. In all of this, argues Brodie, there are intrinsic similarities between the texts, ranging from broad themes to tiny details, which in many cases cannot be accounted for by coincidence. The pattern which emerges is so complex and coherent that deliberate artistry seems to be the only way to account for it. 2 Kgs 5 clearly provides the foundation, although this is not the only Old Testament text lying behind Luke's story at this point (cf. Deut 23.1-2; 29.17; Ps. 77.37; Isa. 58.6), and the story has been told in such a way as to retain fairly close narrative continuity also with the earlier Gospel narrative of Jesus' meeting with the men on the road to Emmaus (Luke 24.13-35).

Here, then, we see that the very way in which the New Testament tells its story depends upon the way in which the story in Kings is itself narrated; and this is not an isolated instance. The general influence of the Elisha stories on the New Testament is well known, and provides the larger context in which to assess the significance of individual examples. Jesus' mission is explicitly paralleled with that of Elisha in Luke 4.27 (what Jesus will do is analogous to what Elisha did when healing Naaman), and the implicit connections are numerous. For example, Jesus heals lepers, just like Elisha (2 Kgs 5; Matt. 8.1-4; 10.8; 11.5; Mark 1.40-45; Luke 5.12-16; 7.22; 17.11-19; cf. also John 9.1-12 for a different kind of healing story which has analogies to the Naaman narrative). He transforms water (2 Kgs 2.19-22; Jn 2.1-11) and suspends the laws of gravity in relation to it (2 Kgs 6.1-7; Mt. 14.22-33; Mk 6.45-51; Jn 6.16-21). He raises the dead (2 Kgs 4.8-37; Mk 5.21-24, 35-43; Lk. 7.11-17; Jn 11.17-37) and multiplies food (2 Kgs 4.1-7, 42-44; Mt. 14.13-21; 15.29-39; Mk 6.30-44; 8.1-10; Lk. 9.10-17; Jn 6.1-15). It seems that some effort has been expended by the New Testament authors in presenting Elisha as a 'type' (pre-figurement) of Christ, perhaps spurred on in particular by the fact that the names 'Elisha' and 'Jesus' have essentially the same meaning ('God saves'). It is not just the Elisha stories which have influenced the telling of the New Testament story in such ways, however, as we shall see shortly.

b. *The Book of Kings as Christian Scripture*
In so far as the book of Kings is regarded as Christian Scripture by its readers, then, it should be taken as *foundational* Christian Scripture, and thus given a much more important place in Christian thinking than has often been the case in the recent past. For extensive sections of Christian history the meaning of Old Testament books in general has commonly been regarded as being entirely bestowed upon them by the New Testament, or at the least it has been 'filtered' through the New Testament (for example by taking the New Testament's explicit use of the Old Testament as the only category of importance in thinking biblical theological thoughts about the latter). This kind of approach to the Old Testament has been tied up with an emphasis on the discontinuity between the testaments, often expressed in terms of a dichotomy, for example, between law and gospel, where the Old Testament is seen largely as 'law' which has been superseded by the New Testament 'gospel'. It is this kind of conviction about the relationship of the testaments which has led to a position where the Old Testament is only read through the lens of New Testament. This is, however, a far from adequate representation of the complex relationship between the testaments, which in overstressing the discontinuity between them has understressed important elements of continuity, and has failed to see the ways in which the Old Testament provides the context in which the New Testament should be read, as well as the reverse. In overstressing discontinuity, indeed, scholars have often actually misrepresented the Old Testament. This is certainly true with regard to the law/gospel dichotomy just referred to, which is based upon a profound misunderstanding of the nature of law in the Old Testament. If the idea that books

like Kings should be regarded as foundational Christian Scripture is to be taken seriously at all, it must mean that they are allowed to speak to the Church with their own voice, in concert with the New Testament rather than in some manner of subordination to it.

That one's attitude to the relationship of the testaments does make a considerable difference to the way in which questions are framed and answered in terms of the exegesis of particular passages is clear if we return for a moment to Brodie's reading of 2 Kings 5 in conjunction with Acts 8. Brodie understands one aspect of the relationship between the passages in this way: the Syrian commander's *physical* renewal in Kings has been adapted in Acts to form the basis for describing the Ethiopian treasurer's *internal* renewal; the deviousness of Gehazi has been adapted to depict the more internal deviation of Simon. It is difficult to see how one could possibly make these kinds of distinctions unless one were already working with a pronounced gospel/law dichotomy of the sort mentioned above, expressed in this instance in terms of what is external (Old Testament) and what is internal (New Testament). For Brodie himself *tells* us elsewhere (1986: 45-46) that the Old Testament story '...tells of an imposing man who, through his servants, came to appreciate what is small and lowly, in other words, who passed from one mentality to another, and who thus was healed'. This is indeed much closer to the mark, in that it links the external washing and healing with the internal transformation of the gentile Naaman who confesses after his washing: 'Behold, I know that there is no God in all the earth but in Israel' (2 Kgs 5.15). One cannot divorce the internal and the external in the case of Naaman, any more than one can do this in the case of the Ethiopian. It is important to realize, indeed, the extent to which the words in 5.12 ('Could I not wash in them and be clean?') evoke the cleansing ritual of Leviticus 13–14 and thus set up a contrast in the story between ritual cleansing and 'real' cleansing. Naaman's complaint is that he came for the latter and has been offered the former instead. His servants, who are better listeners, succeed in undermining this false interpretation of Elisha's words (he spoke only of ritual cleansing) in order that a true interpretation will prevail (he

spoke of a cure, using the language of ritual cleansing). The
whole question of which sort of cleansing is required and on
offer is very much part of the narrative. If one cannot divorce
internal and external in the case of Naaman, however, neither can one plausibly do it in the case of Gehazi, as if his
external deviousness were being expressed in the Kings narrative as quite independent of his internal deviation from
God. It is well worth noting the way in which Gehazi's aspirations to wealth and status are described in 2 Kgs 5.26 precisely in terms which evoke Samuel's warning against
kingship in 1 Sam. 8.14-17, with all its implications of apostasy. The linking of wealth and apostasy is already found
in passages like Deut. 6.10-12. To portray the connections
between Kings and Acts in the way that Brodie has
attempted, then, is in the end (indeed, from the beginning) to
miss the mark. And it is the sort of missing of the mark to
which those who read the New Testament, while not taking
the Old Testament seriously in its own right, seem peculiarly
prone.

The truth of the matter is that it is the continuities
between this story and the New Testament which are most
striking, not the discontinuities. The narrative is replete
with themes which reappear in the later testament. Israel's
God is acknowledged as the only real God there is, the God of
gentile as well as Jew (2 Kgs 5.1, 15; cf. 1 Kgs 8.22-53; 17.17-
24; 18.20-40). This is a God who is prepared to be gracious to
those 'outside the camp' (in this case someone who is not only
a foreigner, but a leper as well), and also to pronounce judgment on 'insiders'. As throughout the Elisha stories, the
humble (the servants, 2 Kgs 5.3, 13) are presented as having
more insight than the exalted (kings, army commanders, 5.1,
6-7); it is they, rather than the exalted, who are the channels
of divine salvation. It is through listening to their words, and
indeed through becoming like them in submitting to authority, in becoming 'as a little child' (5.14), that the exalted come
to know this salvation. The internal transformation is accompanied by the external sign of healing, the water functioning
as the medium of the move from old to new life. It is unneces-
sary to spell out in detail how all these themes reappear
later, are indeed important New Testament themes (cf., e.g.,

Mt. 18.1-5; 19.13-15; Mk 9.33-37; 10.13-16; Lk. 9.46-48;
18.15-17; Jn 3.1-8; Rom. 6.1-5; 1 Cor. 6.11; Col. 2.11-15;
Tit. 3.4-7). There is a high degree of continuity between the
testaments, at both the literary and theological levels.

c. *The Book of Kings in the Light of the New Testament*
It is nevertheless the case that the voice with which the Old
Testament must be allowed to speak to the church is indeed
a voice heard in concert with the New Testament. If the Old
Testament voice should not be permitted to be drowned out
by the New Testament, neither should it be pretended that
Christian hearing of that voice is not profoundly affected by
the context in which it is now heard. Christians are bound to
read a book like Kings in the light of the whole biblical story
as it has unfolded to what (to them) is its end. They are
bound, in particular, to read it in the light of the words and
actions of the central character of that story, Jesus Christ.
They are given clear encouragement to do so by the New
Testament itself, precisely in the way that it weaves the Old
Testament story into its presentation of the gospel which is
centred around the Christ figure. We have already noted the
way in which from the standpoint of the New Testament
Elisha can be seen as functioning typologically in respect of
Jesus; and this is also true of other Old Testament figures.
We may take as a further example here the figure of Solomon.
   Solomon is presented to us in the book of Kings as being
for the most part a wise king, albeit that his wisdom was not
always used for honourable ends (1 Kgs 2.13-46). He was also
for the most part a king who was committed to his God. Yet
even from the start, we are told, there were question marks
about his integrity (1 Kgs 3.1-3 and so on), signs of a way-
ward heart; and eventually his accumulated individual indis-
cretions turned to outright apostasy, as he turned away from
God (1 Kgs 11.1-8). He was in many ways an ideal king ruling over an ideal kingdom; but ideal and reality were always
in some degree of tension, and eventually the reality was
much less than the ideal. He was, most of all, a king blessed
by God. Solomon consistently believed that the blessing of
God, and particularly the blessing of an eternal dynasty, was
in the first instance tied up with moral virtue—his father's

and his own. That is what David had himself told him (1 Kgs
2.2-4); and that is what God had seemingly confirmed to him
(1 Kgs 9.3-9). Blessing in fact continued even through indis-
cretion, however; and eventually it appeared (1 Kgs 11), as
readers of 2 Samuel 7 might well have suspected, that there
was more to God's dealings with David's house than David
had told his son. God's punishment of this house would not
be as severe, initially, as might have been expected (1 Kgs
11.12-13, 32, 34, 36); and that even such punishment as had
befallen was not eternal (1 Kgs 11.39). *God's* choice was in
the end indeed to be more important than human choices,
even if mortals could never presume on grace in order to
evade the demands of law. Such a hopeful ending to the
Solomon story carries with it the implication that there can
also be hope (the hope expressed in Solomon's own prayer of
1 Kgs 8.22-53) at the end of Israel's story, when the as-yet-
unfulfilled threats of 1 Kgs 9.6-9 finally become realities
(2 Kgs 24–25). For if David's son is always to sit on the
throne, God must forgive; a throne must be restored upon
which he may sit; and a people must be reconstituted over
which he may rule.

The idea of an eternal throne for the son of David is an idea
which the New Testament picks up and develops. Here Jesus
is identified as *the* Son of David towards whom the Davidic
promise ultimately points (Mt. 1.1-16; 21.1-11; 22.41-46), *the*
king who sits upon David's throne (Lk. 1.32-33; Jn 18.28-40;
Acts 2.29-36). He is the one greater than Solomon, fulfilling
the messianic promise of Isa. 11.1-9 (with its backward glance
at Solomon in vv. 2-3), to whose wisdom people should listen,
as the Queen of Sheba had listened to Solomon (Mt. 12.42;
Lk. 11.31; cf. also Mt. 13.54; Lk. 2.40, 52). Like the wisdom
teachers of the Old Testament Jesus is often to be found in
the gospels encouraging his hearers to learn about God by
observing how God's world works (e.g. Mt. 6.25-34; Lk. 12.22-
34). More than that, however, the New Testament presents
him to us as himself the *incarnation* of wisdom, the very
Wisdom of God (1 Cor. 1.24), present with the Father from
the beginning of Creation (Jn 1.1-18; Col. 1.15-20; cf. Prov.
3.19-20; 8.22-31). Jesus supersedes Solomon, not least in the
fact that in Jesus wisdom and obedience to law are perfectly

integrated (Rom. 5.19; Heb. 5.8), whereas in Solomon they were always in tension and ultimately divorced. Solomon, conversely, points forward typologically to Jesus. Once this is seen, it is difficult to read the Solomon story without echoes of the Jesus story sounding in one's ears (e.g. in the 'coronation' scene of 1 Kgs 1.38-40; cf. Mt. 21.1-11).

All the Old Testament characters who prefigure Jesus are presented in the Christian Bible as less than the ideal towards whom they point. Even David had deficiencies, as Matthew's genealogy of Jesus somewhat brutally reminds the reader (Mt. 1.6) in referring to Bathsheba, not by name, but as 'Uriah's wife'. There is plenty of evidence of Solomon's deficiencies in 1 Kings 1–11, not least in his attitude towards his renowned wealth towards the end of his reign, where the text suggests that all was not well. It is interesting in view of the seeming ambivalence of Kings on this point that the only reference to Solomon's 'splendour' in the New Testament occurs in a section of Jesus' teaching (recorded in slightly differing forms in Mt. 6.25-34 and Lk. 12.22-31) which seeks to encourage Christians not to allow concern about material needs to interfere with the seeking of God's kingdom. Both gospels associate this teaching with other teaching about 'not storing up treasures on earth', but in heaven, lest the heart go astray (Mt. 6.19-21; Lk. 12.32-34); and Luke makes the issue doubly clear by associating the teaching also with the parable of the rich fool (Lk. 12.13-21) and with the injunction to 'sell your possessions and give to the poor' (Lk. 12.33). The emphasis in these texts on God's provision of the *necessities* of life and on the imperative to *share* wealth with others is particularly interesting when one considers the emphasis in 1 Kgs 9.10–10.29 on Solomon's *extravagance* and apparent *self-absorption*. We even have a token pagan 'running after these things' (Mt. 6.32; Lk. 12.30) in the shape of the Queen of Sheba.

In this last example Solomon can be seen as functioning not so much as a type of Christ, but as a warning and example to the New Testament believer. If from the standpoint of the New Testament the characters of the Old Testament can be understood as prefiguring Christ, so also can they be understood as providing models for Christian behaviour.

This is consistent with the New Testament view of the purpose of a book like Kings, that it does not tell us about Israel's past so that we should become better informed about it in some abstract, intellectually detached way, but so that we should learn from it (Rom. 15.4; 1 Cor. 10.11; 2 Tim. 3.16-17). It is consequently the case that a theme can be picked up from an earlier story and used in exhortatory or pastoral fashion in relation to later generations. This is true not only of Solomon but also, for example, of Elijah. Christians can learn valuable lessons from Elijah's life, the New Testament writers affirm—whether about the way in which God works with 'remnants' of his people (Rom. 11.1-6; the remnant theme is an important one throughout Kings); or faith (Heb. 11.32-39); or prayer (Jas. 5.13-18). Taking a lead from such uses of the book of Kings, it would be possible to pick up other themes and pursue them within the Christian Bible as a whole in the same way.

The 'wisdom of Solomon' theme is certainly one which could usefully be pursued, since the exploration of the nature of wisdom which is found in 1 Kings 1–11 is also found in the New Testament. As pointed out already, Jesus himself exhorted people to 'read nature' as a way of finding out about God and his ways (cf. 1 Kgs 4.33-34 [MT 5.13-14]). He was also known to commend a worldly-wise attitude to the world, as in Mt. 10.16, 'be as shrewd as snakes and as innocent as doves': Solomon, it might be argued, was good at playing the snake, if not quite so convincing as the dove (1 Kgs 2). As far as wisdom in administration is concerned (1 Kgs 4–5), the New Testament is plainly in favour of it (e.g. Acts 6.3). Yet the New Testament is, like the Solomon story, well aware of the inadequacies of and dangers inherent in a wisdom which is simply 'from below'. The New Testament authors know that it can express itself as idle words and empty philosophy, if not as outright apostasy and 'freedom' from God's law (e.g. Rom. 1.21-25; Col. 2.8; Jas. 3.13-18). And there is a strong line of thought running right throughout the New Testament which concerns the inability of the 'wise' of themselves to hear the Gospel (e.g. 1 Cor. 1.18-25). True wisdom must be revealed 'from above'; and it is characteristically revealed to 'children' (Lk. 10.21)—to those who are not wise by worldly standards at all (e.g. 1 Cor. 1.26-31). Wisdom 'from above' is thus given the same central place in the New Testament as it is in the Solomon story (1 Kgs 3), where it, too, is wisdom which is revealed to 'a little child' who knows his need (3.7)— wisdom which leads on to wise judgment (cf. the expectation of 1 Cor. 6.5).

These are just a few examples of the way the book of Kings is read in the New Testament as Scripture and might be read by Christians as Scripture in accordance with the general perspective which the New Testament adopts. These examples demonstrate well the way in which the Christian hearing of the Old Testament voice is indeed profoundly affected by the context in which it is now heard. Christians are bound to read a book like Kings in the light of the whole biblical story as it has unfolded to its end. It is simply inevitable that they will do so; indeed one might well put it more strongly, and assert that it is theologically essential that they do so. Seen in the context of the Christian Bible the story of Kings can be perceived as functioning typologically in respect of the later New Testament story, preparing its way and gaining full significance only when read with it in mind, as readers attach their own story to the larger biblical narrative whole and understand themselves in its context.

Further Reading

On Scripture and canon:

J. Barr, *Holy Scripture: Canon, Authority, Criticism* (Oxford: Clarendon Press, 1983).

J. Barton, *Oracles of God: Perceptions of Ancient Prophecy in Israel After the Exile* (London: Darton, Longman and Todd, 1986). Further development of the basic ideas found in Barr.

R. Beckwith, *The Old Testament Canon of the New Testament Church and its Background in Early Judaism* (London: SPCK, 1985). A voluminous reassertion of a more traditional view of the canon.

R. Beckwith, 'A modern theory of the Old Testament canon', *VT* 41 (1991), pp. 385-95. A detailed critique of Barton's position.

B.S. Childs, *Introduction to the Old Testament as Scripture* (London: SCM Press, 1979), pp. 27-106.

B.S. Childs, *Biblical Theology of the Old and New Testaments: Theological Reflection on the Christian Bible* (Minneapolis: Fortress Press, 1993), pp. 3-94.

R. Smend, 'Questions About the Importance of the Canon in an Old Testament Introduction', *JSOT* 16 (1980), pp. 45-51.

On reading the Old Testament/Tanak from within a religious tradition:
J.D. Levenson, *The Hebrew Bible, the Old Testament and Historical Criticism: Jews and Christians in Biblical Studies* (Louisville: Westminster/John Knox, 1993).
F. Watson, *Text, Church and World: Biblical Interpretation in Theological Perspective* (Edinburgh: T. & T. Clark, 1994).

On the relationship between the Old Testament and New Testament in general:
D.L. Baker, *Two Testaments, One Bible: A Study of the Theological Relationship between the Old and New Testaments* (Leicester: Apollos, rev. edn, 1991).
J. Goldingay, *Approaches to Old Testament Interpretation* (ICT; Leicester: Inter-Varsity Press, rev. edn, 1990).
L. Goppelt, *Typos: The Typological Interpretation of the Old Testament in the New* (Grand Rapids: Eerdmans, 1982).

On the ways in which the New Testament story has been shaped by the Old Testament generally and Kings in particular:
T.L. Brodie, 'Towards Unraveling the Rhetorical Imitation of Sources in Acts: 2 Kgs 5 as One Component of Acts 8,9-40', *Bib* 67 (1986), pp. 41-67.
I.W. Provan, *1 and 2 Kings*, passim.
W.M. Swartley, *Israel's Scripture Traditions and the Synoptic Gospels: Story Shaping Story* (Peabody, MA: Hendrickson, 1994). Note especially the helpful review of previous contributions on this topic on pp. 9-31.

On the Bible as a single book:
G. Josipovici, *The Book of God: A Response to the Bible* (Newhaven, CT and London: Yale University Press, 1988).

Indexes

Index of References

Old Testament

Genesis		31.26	24	15.1	22
37–50	74			18	19
		Joshua			
Exodus		1.6-9	24	*1 Kings*	
1.14	42	1.7	24	1–11	86, 115,
2.23	42	1.8	24		116
4.1-17	42	8.30-35	24	1–2	18-20,
4.21	42	23.6	24		23, 30
5.1-21	42	24.26	24	1	19, 21,
7.3-4	42				22
7.13	42	*1 Samuel*		1.1–2.11	83
20	86	4.9	24	1.1-4	22
20.4	42	8.11	22	1.1	27
32	79	8.14-17	112	1.5-6	22
32.1-35	42	9.2	23	1.13-30	22
32.4	42	10.23-24	23	1.13	22
32.5	42, 71	16.7	23	1.14	22
32.26	42, 71	17	23	1.17	22
		25	22	1.29	22
Leviticus		25.3	22	1.30	22
13–14	111	31	19	1.38-40	115
				1.51	22
Deuteronomy		*2 Samuel*		2	19, 116
4.15-24	78	2.8	21	2.1-4	24, 87
4.29	24	7	88, 114	2.2-4	114
6.2	24	7.1-17	19	2.3-4	24
6.10-12	112	7.12-13	19	2.3	24, 75
8.6	24	7.12	19	2.4	88
9.5	24	7.14-16	88	2.10-11	20
11.1	24	7.15-16	93	2.12–11.43	83
12	71	11	19, 22	2.12	19
12.1-7	75	11.2	22	2.13-46	113
17.18-20	75	11.6-27	19	3	19, 117
17.20	75	12	19	3.1-3	113
23.1-2	109	12.1-12	19	3.2-14	77
28.61	24	12.15-23	19	3.2-3	55, 56
29.9	24	13–18	23	3.2	86
29.17	109	13	19	3.3-14	23
29.21	24	14.20	22	3.7	117
30.10	24	14.25-26	23	4–5	116

INDEX OF AUTHORS